THE MOUNTAIN
THE MINER
AND THE
LORD

Harry M. Caudill

THE MOUNTAIN THE MINER AND THE LORD

and Other Tales from a Country Law Office

THE UNIVERSITY PRESS OF KENTUCKY

LIBRARY OF CONGRESS CATALOGING IN PUBLICATION DATA

Caudill, Harry M   1922-
  The mountain, the miner, and the Lord, and other tales from
a country law office.

  CONTENTS: A visit to the White House.—Little
Thuggie.—The mountain, the miner, and the Lord.—[etc.]
    1. Letcher Co., Ky.—Social life and customs—Addresses,
essays, lectures.   2. Letcher Co., Ky.—Biography—
Addresses, essays, lectures.   3. Kentucky—Social life and
customs—Addresses, essays, lectures. 4. Kentucky—
Biography—Addresses, essays, lectures. 5. Caudill, Harry M.,
1922-   —Addresses, essays, lectures.   I. Title.
F457.L48C38   976.9'163   80-51012
ISBN 0-8131-1403-9

Scholarly publisher for the Commonwealth,
serving Berea College, Centre College of Kentucky,
Eastern Kentucky University, The Filson Club,
Georgetown College, Kentucky Historical Society,
Kentucky State University, Morehead State University,
Murray State University, Northern Kentucky University,
Transylvania University, University of Kentucky,
University of Louisville, and Western Kentucky University.

Editorial and Sales Offices: Lexington, Kentucky 40506

Contents

Preface

Lyndon Johnson loved to speak of the United States as the "richest and most powerful country in the history of the world." It was obvious from the context of his speeches that he measured riches in money, in agricultural bounty and manufacturing capacity—the ability to turn out myriads of material things. In this respect America is rich, but this is a faulty standard for measuring the wealth and well-being of a nation.

I had the good fortune to be born in 1922 in Letcher County, Kentucky. This event, so important to me, occurred in an old-fashioned and altogether modest house in a tiny hollow called the Long Branch of the Kentucky River. The Kentucky hills were a fascinating place in which to grow to manhood.

As I grew up, the thin layer of topsoil on which six generations of farmers had depended for subsistence was wearing out and being washed down the rivers to the sea. Huge numbers of people were coming in from other states and from Europe to labor in the scores of coal mines that had opened since 1910. Thousands of native-born mountaineers were simultaneously shaking the dust of their hills from their shoes and heading north, west, and south—the beginning of mammoth out-migration that eventually carried more than a million of them to lives in strange new surroundings. Most local travel was still afoot or on horseback, but cars were becoming more common. Roads were abominable but the people had caught the highway fever, and construction was under way. Telephones were largely unknown outside the towns, and the suave voice of the radio announcer was just beginning to intrude into mountain households.

Homes were heated by fireplaces and stoves. Only the wealthy had furnaces and plumbing. Schools were mostly one-room affairs and teachers were paid about seventy-five dollars monthly for a seven- or eight-month term. College degrees were almost unknown. Discipline was strict and misconduct brought thrashings which parents usually duplicated at the end of the day.

The Bible was the source of nearly all wisdom, and even confirmed "sinners" said they believed every word of it. It was taught in the schools, and the day began with a prayer. No one supposed for a moment that any of this was unconstitutional. Patriotism was the second religion of the hill people. "God and Country" and "My Country Right or Wrong" were printed by childish hands on countless sheets of pulp tablet paper.

Society was largely patriarchal. Families clustered about the "old people," with sons, daughters, sons-in-law, daughters-in-law, and grandchildren looking to them for advice in matters of morals, marriage, economics, and politics. The grandparents were a living cement that held the generations together and provided for the transmission of folk information. Along with the stories of people and things from other days, and the title to the shrinking bits of land, were transmitted immense amounts of folk knowledge. In the hills a young man grew up as a passable rough carpenter who could "frame out" a house or barn. He could take off a worn sole and repair his shoes on a last that might have been old when the rebels fired on Fort Sumter. He could plow, plant, and harvest a dozen varieties of garden vegetables and knew the season when each task should be done. He knew the trees and the low ground-plants of his native hills and could brew tonics and teas that lessened pain and supplied needed vitamins and minerals. He was an adequate smith, and might be able to "draw iron" and fashion it into tools, hinges, and even guns. He could slaughter hogs and cattle, preserve the meat, and tan the hides. He was a skilled hunter, knew the haunts and hiding places of birds and animals, and could emulate their calls with amazing fidelity. His fingers produced dulcimers and banjos, and brought forth tunes to accompany the ancient songs which his imagination embellished and enlarged. In the mines he could set roof props, drill blast-holes, charge them with explosives, set off the "shots," and then "clean up the cut." He might still remember how to boil niter from sandstone and mix it with hard maple charcoal and sulfur boiled from "powder water" to compound highly potent black powder.

In many of these tasks, his wife worked alongside him. She could also clip wool from the back of a sheep, clean it, comb it, card it, and dye it. The ability to spin it into thread and weave it into patterned cloth had not been wholly lost. She knew how to trim the fat from the guts of hogs and transform it into soap. She could preserve foods by drying, canning, and pickling, and brew remedies from a score of plants. Her "granny woman" often did a creditable job of delivering her babies.

Frugality was a perpetual and instinctive part of living. All in all, they were a profoundly knowledgeable people. They were also grossly ignorant. They doubted that the world was round and were familiar only with the theory that it was about six thousand years old, having been made with all its creatures in precisely six days. Most of them could read little or nothing, and not one house in a dozen subscribed to any reading matter. To their sorrow they knew nothing at all about cover-cropping and crop rotation. Superstitions were rampant. The notion that germs caused sickness was only slowly gaining acceptance, and sanitary standards were shockingly low by today's norms. But when all this is conceded they still knew a tremendous lot.

When they are compared to their descendants of the same age today it seems likely that a great shrinkage of overall information has occurred. Today's young can read appreciably better but most get their "news"—the information by which they live— from the inanities and pomposities of television. They have a smattering of general information that is impressive, but are shockingly weak on specifics. The skills of their forebears have been lost. If cast onto the land or into an industrial city they arrive without skills. They may laugh at the ignorance of their ancestors, but in a very real sense they are vastly more ignorant. They tend to be unemployable generalists who can earn no bread until a narrow and specific aptitude is acquired. Compare the knowledge of the hill farmer of 1927—who perforce lived by the skills I have referred to—with that of his grandson who spends his days bolting rear bumpers onto Ford cars, and the limitation of the latter is chilling.

Or consider the grandmother who spun, dyed, wove, sewed, made soap, preserved and cooked food she had grown, milked her cow, and saw to a thousand details without visiting a store. Is her granddaughter—who lives in an all-electric mobile home and feeds her baby a canned milk formula, her husband a frozen, prepacked dinner bought at the A & P—as wise or knowing a person?

I practiced law within a mile of my birthplace for twenty-eight years and saw and talked to a daily procession of people. In them were mirrored the changes and shifts that transformed a culture and people. Roads went up the creeks and hollows, and the isolated and landlocked became mobile. Schools were consolidated, and the precinct and community lost importance. Out-migration reduced populations by half and shattered the patriarchies. The honored old became "senior citizens" shut up in nursing homes. Public Assistance expanded to provide livings as good as the old order could wrest from the thinning soil, and neither government nor industry provided new skills or significant jobs. Television absorbed huge portions of each day and the ancient folk music and the other arts of self-entertainment dwindled away. The man whose father built his home with axe, hammer, and saw bought his own complete from a mobile-home vendor. New attitudes and insights entered the schools, and discipline evaporated.

The old, rough self-reliance bequeathed by the frontier yielded to an idle and vapid materialism. In a real sense the people were decultured. Rapid and gigantic changes engulfed, overwhelmed, and transformed them. The new mountaineer became, in the main, a rootless individual cut off from his cultural origins, his beginnings, his heritage.

A culture is comparable to the floor of a forest. The first layer is made up of clearly recognizable leaves from the most recent autumn. The next layer is less recognizable, the one after that formless, and finally there is a rich mass of unremembered mold from remote times. But the plant atop this composition grows out of it all, is nourished by it all, and contributes to it all. The composite layer is the plant's heritage.

A culture is accumulated in the same manner, an accretion deposited by each generation. Six or eight generations back, the deposits become formless, but the influences persist. We cannot escape the consequences of what those old dead generations did and left to us. Daily we confront in others, and ourselves act out, influences whose social beginnings were old in Europe when Caesar's legions sailed for Britain.

These tales are intended to show how the cultural layers were formed and a people fashioned. That culture and people are vanishing and a radically new culture is rising on their ruin.

Television and peripatetic mobility are the principal deculturing influences that have ravaged the mores of the central Appalachians. These influences have been greatly aided by the impact of a gigantic, resurgent coal industry and the simultaneous growth of the welfare state. What will become of the new mountaineer in his plastic house trailer or, if he is a prosperous coal operator, in his flimsy new demi-mansion? That story must be left for others to tell and for other listeners to hear. We can be sure, however, that the forces of change will continue to work, that good and bad times will follow one another, that poor men will become rich and rich men will become poor, that great challenges will confront the human spirit, and that survival will depend on struggle and courage.

These tales have come from the people and the land. The land shapes the people, and the people shape the land. The cycle is perpetual and the results are dramatic and sometimes frightening.

Throughout the years I tried to hear the drama on the tongues of the people and see it in their hands and faces. The people afforded me a good living and I tried to afford them a good listener. The sorrow, courage, tragedy, and achievement of their days deserve a better record. It is a pity that so much of their story must remain unchronicled because for a long time there have been few who were willing to hear and encourage when men and women brimmed with stories to be told.

Most of the people whose stories I have told are dead, but as long as I survive I shall hear their steps upon my stair, feel the grip of their hands upon my own, have my life brightened by the memory of their smiles, and thrill again and again to the tales they told in my country law office.

Their legacy was rich beyond anything President Johnson had in mind.

A Visit to
the White House

THROUGHOUT his lifetime Lilley Cornett did almost exactly as he pleased, sometimes to the amusement and often to the outrage of his neighbors. His huge frame, immense work-roughened hands, and craggy features were of a kind the Dutch masters preserved for us on their marvelous canvases of peasants, merchants, and rakes. Like so many of Rembrandt's subjects, Lilley Cornett was utterly self-assured. He wasted little time on considerations of right and wrong but aimed only to get what he wanted, and to do so in the most direct and practical manner.

Lilley was born and grew up on Line Fork Creek, a thirty-nine-mile-long tributary that joins the Kentucky River midway between the county seat towns of Whitesburg and Hazard. His forebear, William Cornett, came with Gideon Ison and Gudgeon Ingram from North Carolina in the 1790s, and the three became the valley's first settlers. The stream took its name from the fact that a party of surveyors had been there before the settlers and had left the marks of their axes on a long line of the mammoth trees that grew in profusion from creek bank to hilltop. By Lilley's time the population had grown to a couple of thousand, a figure that would be abruptly halved by the out-migration triggered by World War II.

The long, sinuous valley was virtually roadless until the 1950s when the state built a "rural highway" to precincts and communities called Hallie, Turkey Creek, Skyline, Defeated Creek, Banks, Trace Fork, Bear Branch, Big Branch, Ingram's

Creek, Gordon, and Gilley. Such "roads" as the county provided generally ran in the creek bed and were practically impassable. Thus Lilley lived out his days in backwoods isolation, little affected by the uproar that daily filled the columns of urban newspapers.

When he returned from the army after World War I he worked for several years as a coal miner at Seco. Coal prices were high and Southeast Coal Company paid substantial wages. He saved "nearly every cent" he earned, living almost entirely on potatoes, meal, and salt bacon he brought from his parents' farm to the company's boardinghouse for bachelor miners. Land was cheap along the Line Fork and there were eager sellers anxious to move to industrial jobs in Ohio and Michigan, so Lilley's mining money was exchanged for some fertile bottomland and approximately 400 acres of steep hillsides. Much of this more rugged land was still in virgin stands of tulip poplar, oak, beech, hickory, and gum. Nearly all other timber stands in the area had been acquired by W. M. Ritter Lumber Company and American Column and Lumber Company, but Lilley guarded the title to his acres with unwavering fidelity. When the lumber demands of a new war sent the huge trees crashing down elsewhere, Lilley's forest stood tall and safe. As he observed, "As long as I live, I aim to be able to look out and see them big trees a-growin'." (They survived his death and in 1969 the state bought the land as a nature preserve. Thousands of scientists, students, and just plain nature lovers come each year to visit the unique survival of climax forest and intricate ground cover known as "Lilley's Woods.")

After his mining days, Lilley married a comely young neighbor named Polly Ann Griffith. She bore him several children and came to be known to them, to the community generally, and, in her old age, to many visitors in Lilley's Woods, as "Ma." Ma Cornett was an exemplary wife and deserved only the most exemplary treatment from her hard-headed husband—treatment which was not always forthcoming.

2

As Lilley confided to me, "One woman ain't hardly enough fer a man if he is any account a-tall." As Lilley related the tales, this conviction got him into serious trouble when he was about thirty, and Ma and his growing brood had begun to pall somewhat. He cast about for diversion and became enamored of a handsome young widow who lived on Cutshin Creek in Leslie County. He conducted a clandestine courtship that resulted in a pledge of marriage as soon as Ma could be divorced.

Never one to allow legal niceties to stand in his way, Lilley moved quickly to secure the coveted decree. He took his bride-to-be to a lawyer at Hazard, told the attorney that he lived on Big Leatherwood Creek in Perry County, and with a straight face introduced his intended bride as his present wife. He explained that he and his wife had no children, owned no property, and mutually desired to end the marriage. The unsuspecting counselor drew up a petition and separation agreement which Lilley and his lady friend promptly signed and swore to be true in all respects. On the basis of these fraudulent documents a divorce judgment was entered of record, and Ma was astounded when Lilley handed her a certified copy of the court's decree ending their marriage and restoring each of them to "the status of a single and unmarried person." Lilley told her that she had to leave and that he would take care of the children. Ma returned to her parents' cabin, and Lilley set about the task of bringing in a new bride.

As his plans proceeded, he was disconcerted to learn that Ma was taking her expulsion from his hearth and home with unbecoming equanimity. He was pleased, of course, that she had not gone to a lawyer and sued to set aside the flagrantly illegal judgment. As he had anticipated, her illiteracy, her total lack of experience with courts and county seats, and her destitution had combined to preclude any such effort on her part. But his gratification on this account was more than nullified by Ma's lack of heartbreak. As a matter of fact, rumors began to reach Lilley that she had found favor in the eyes of a certain widower who lived a few miles down the creek, and that she fully reciprocated his ardent feelings. Indeed, when Lilley announced to his numerous brothers and sisters that his remarriage would take place on a certain day, he learned that on the same day Ma would become the wife of a man Lilley was coming to view with deep distaste.

Lilley's sisters-in-law "spread a big dinner" and after the festivities were over he was left alone with his bride. In due time darkness came on, the children were hustled off to their repose, and Lilley conducted his new wife to the bed so recently and abruptly vacated by the old. Soon thereafter, as Lilley phrased it, "I discovered that I had made one hell of a bad swap!" Set aflame by the knowledge that the hour was growing late at Ma's new household he sprang from the bed, put on his clothes, grabbed a lantern and pistol, and "took off along a nigh way" to rescue her from her peril. Arriving at the darkened house he banged and kicked on the door until the startled groom opened the door and gazed wrathfully out into the small space illumined by the pale rays of the lantern.

Lilley stuck the muzzle of the pistol under his rival's nose and pushed past him into the house. "By God, I got there just barely in the nick of time," he later recalled, a fortunate circumstance that enabled him to rouse Ma out of the warm bed and lead her by twisting paths through dark woods to her rightful home. The children were delighted to have their mother returned to them, and a little after daybreak the unsatisfactory wife of eighteen hours was hustled back to her indignant kinsmen in Leslie County. Life returned to its old routines with all concerned much happier after the upheaval. Ma's would-be husband accepted the abrupt reordering of his arrangements without visible discontent, but the widow from Cutshin proved to be a different proposition. Precisely nine months after her hectic wedding night she was delivered of a superb baby boy, whom about three weeks later, she handed to the startled father. Lilley was not unhappy to have another pair of lungs howling for food and, besides, the unexpected heir was "mighty cute." Ma took up the task of diaper and bottle with her customary patience and the boy grew up

4

with his half brothers and sisters, fully accepted and equally loved.

In later years when the boys and girls were all grown and one of them had made his way through college, the last of Letcher County's great trees had gone to the mills—excepting only those in Lilley's Woods. The tireless cutters and loggers had felled not only the huge primal trees but had returned for the second growth and sawed it into roof props for eastern Kentucky's innumerable mines. The once-glorious forest had been reduced to a ragged remnant composed of damaged and cull trees and broad expanses of cleared, burnt-over land that had reverted to sawbriers and broom sage. Still the nation's lust for sound hardwoods was unabated and numerous timber agents made their way to Lilley's door.

Sam Collins was a distinguished-looking, silver-haired trafficker and trader who lived at Whitesburg. He had once been Prohibition Director for Kentucky and Tennessee, and as such he had helped send Congressman "Big John" Langley of Pikeville to a federal penitentiary for violation of the Volstead Act, a role for which many Republicans—including Lilley—never forgave him. One bright May morning in 1954, when the rays of an early sun glistened on the dewdrops along the tops of Lilley's beloved trees, he suddenly perceived a way to bring a long-delayed punishment to Sam Collins for his infidelity to the Republican congressman who had obtained his appointment as chief revenuer. At the same time, he could acquire some much needed information at absolutely no cost to himself.

The next day Lilley caught a ride to the county seat and found Mr. Collins loafing in his accustomed spot in front of the Daniel Boone Hotel. Approaching him with a wide, toothy grin and outstretched hand Lilley electrified Collins. "Sam," he said, "I've been a-thinkin' about you a lot, and about what good Republicans we have always been together down through the years. You've been a good friend to me and now I want to be a good friend to you."

5

Collins glowed and Lilley continued, "I'm a-thinkin' to sell my timber and I don't know how to go about hit. You've been around a sight and know people in Louis-ville and all sorts of places, and I want you to sell the timber for me, and make yerself some money, too, when you do hit. I'll sell hit to you at the right kind of price, and I'll appreciate hit a sight in this world if you will help me out so I won't lose my shirt on the deal."

Collins agreed to help Lilley—in fact, to make a special effort in his old friend's behalf. He bought Lilley's lunch at the hotel dining room and, as soon as his guest turned homeward, rushed to a telephone to call Wood Mosaic Corporation at Louisville. The gentlemen at that venerable firm were ecstatic at the news that Cornett had weakened and was prepared to sell. It was promptly agreed that Sam would get a written option signed at the earliest possible date; then Wood Mosaic would advance funds to consummate the deal. The walnut would go for furniture and veneering. The white oak would be sold to Seagram for whiskey-barrel staves, and there were numerous other promising possibilities besides.

The next morning Collins paid an attorney to draft a loophole-free option and, with the document in his pocket, departed for Line Fork. He went out of his way a few miles to pick up some ice-cold beer for Lilley at a whiskey store just beyond the Perry County line. He found Lilley safely at home, supremely affable, and warmly grateful for the beer. But when Collins cleared his throat and presented the option, Lilley demurred ever so slightly. Yes, he would sign, of course. The deal was just the thing he had in mind and he was much obliged for what his old friend had done, but still there was one little detail that ought to be attended to first. He thought the timber ought to be "cruised," the trees counted and listed according to their varieties and the board-foot yield of each tree calculated. This was done frequently, of course—was customary in fact—and the disappointed Collins had to suppress his eagerness and frustration while hastening to call Louisville for the services of an experienced timber cruiser.

The cruiser arrived a couple of days later and Sam introduced him to the amiable Lilley, who pointed out his boundary lines and appointed his two oldest sons to accompany him and make sure no trees were omitted. The cruiser began with the huge "spruce pines" at the mouth of Big Everage Branch and with Lilley's sons at his heels began entering the trees in his journal. Each was noted separately as to kind and quality, with an estimate of its board-footage.

For seven days the cruiser clambered about Lilley's Woods, from the deepest hollow to the highest ridgetop. One by one the trees were noted: the lordly tulips, the magnificent white oaks, the immense white and red beeches, the red and black oaks along the upper terraces, the tall straight hickories with their bark falling off in huge shaggy scales, the maples, the sourwoods, the sweet and black gums, the "wahoos" with their gigantic leaves and huge, stinking blossoms, the hornbeams, and the pines. The cruiser knew them all, counted them all, and sized all of them up with an eye that knew within a few planks how much they would yield. When his labors were finished, he dragged himself down from the remotest hilltop, smoked a couple of pipefuls of Prince Albert on Lilley's front porch, and gratefully drained one of the tall cans of cool Schlitz with which Collins had continued to ply Lilley throughout the memorable week. The old mountaineer was delighted that the task had been finished in so thorough and competent a manner and assured Collins that the trade would soon be completed and the trees would start crashing down.

A day was appointed for the matter of the final sale to be taken up and agreed upon, but before Collins drove away, Lilley mentioned one final detail. "Sam," he said, "take that journal book and git a typewriter clerk to type hit all out real good and neat. List just how many of each kind of tree I've got, and how many board feet of each kind, and bring me a copy and then we'll git down to business and wind this whole thing up." He nudged Collins in the rib with a great bony elbow and confided, "I'm agoin' to see that you come outta this in real good shape because of all the trouble and cost you've been put to. I don't need much money myself, but a man like you needs a whole lot and I aim fer you to git hit." Collins sighed with relief and drove away in quest of a "typewriter clerk."

The computations and the typing required a couple of days and the result was several pages of neatly typed lines properly done up in a protective blue manuscript cover. The document was a complete inventory of Lilley's Woods, down to the last tree fit for sale for any purpose, together with excellent estimates as to the amount of salable wood of each type. There were three copies and Collins folded one, put it in an envelope for Lilley, and set out for the farmhouse overlooking the willow-lined banks of Line Fork Creek. He picked up another half dozen frosty cans of beer and handed them to Lilley just as the hot morning sun had begun to instill an inordinate thirst for something cold, sudsy, and ripe with the flavor of malt. Lilley's huge teeth gleamed in a wide grin as he opened one can and handed the rest to one of his boys, admonishing him to put them in the springhouse. He then settled into a sagging rocker, fished his eyeglasses out of a frayed pocket, and spent a quarter of an hour studying the long tally of his trees. Satisfied at last, he returned the spectacles to his pocket and handed the document to the same son with directions to take it in the house and "put hit in the cedar chest." With these details out of the way he turned to the old revenuer, but now the smile was gone.

Gone, too, was the joviality of the last two weeks. Now his jaw was set and his eyes were narrowed and cold. "Sam Collins," he said flatly, "I'm a man of few words and I'll make you one proposition—take hit or leave hit. My price is one million dollars cash before a single tree is cut!" Collins began to sputter in chagrin and disbelief, and to stammer that such a price was completely unreasonable. But Lilley put a stop to further palaver by turning his back and walking into the house, leaving a red-faced, speechless Sam Collins to glare after him, then dash to his car for a wrathful and empty-handed drive to Whitesburg.

As Lilley sipped from a fresh can of beer he contemplated the

8

events of the preceding two weeks with much satisfaction. His stratagem had gotten him all the free beer he could drink—no small consideration in Lilley's frugal mind. It had gained for him a complete inventory of all his trees, a document "worth a thousand dollars in any man's gold." Finally, and of much importance, he had effectively chastised a man for whom he had long nourished a secret dislike. Justice, Lilley calculated, had been done without his having to spend so much as a penny. The beer was especially good when savored at the end of such an eminently successful undertaking.

These episodes in the life of Lilley Cornett are provided simply as an introduction to the man himself, for without some comprehension of this remarkable mountaineer the story he told me on a snowy January morning can scarcely be appreciated. Lilley knocked the snow off his "gum boots," shed his heavy jacket, and explained his problem. He had been born long before systematic birth records were kept in the Kentucky hills and was having trouble providing proof of his exact age. The oldest census record showed him to be two years younger than he had supposed himself to be, and the Social Security Administration had, accordingly, ruled him ineligible for retirement benefits. Lilley wanted me to help him set the record straight because, as he put it, "my little old war pension ain't hardly enough to git by on."

We put together a bulky file in contradiction of the census excerpt. It included some old school records, a photocopy of the birth record preserved in his father's worn Bible, the record of his marriage to "Ma," the census report for 1920, and a certified copy of his discharge from the army in 1919. All supported Lilley's contention and the agency eventually reversed itself and started the monthly checks to his battered mailbox. It was his comments about his army discharge that set me to wondering.

According to Lilley it certified that he had faithfully executed his duties in the Great War and was discharged with honor. He had been at Walter Reed Hospital in Washington at the time, and the document bore the signature of a major acting in behalf of the adjutant general. But there was more. Along the margin at the bottom, someone had typed the words "Discharged by Order of the President," and this curious notation was followed by the signature of a brigadier general—the commandant of the hospital.

Suspecting that this might lead to a story, I asked for an explanation. Lilley looked at me with an unfathomable expression compounded of good humor, imperturbability, slyness, and a vast capacity for deceit. He was a great trader who made much of his living dealing in horses, mules, cattle, hogs, hides, ginseng, and anything else for which he could find a market, and as such he always wore a mask that veiled the thoughts behind his twinkling blue eyes. Those eyes smiled quixotically as he explained how that singular typewritten line and signature "come to be on that there discharge."

The battle of Argonne Forest was, as Lilley put it, a mighty unhealthy commotion for a strapping lad from the hills to find himself in. The Germans were fighting hard, and one morning when the Yanks went over the top Lilley was "shot square through twice." The perforations of his stomach and guts came close to ending his career then and there, and it was a mighty close-run thing for several weeks after, but Lilley was "tough as whang leather" and gradually fought his way back from the brink of the grave. The armistice found him in a ward at Walter Reed Hospital, his wounds healed but his midsection still tremulous. The doctors treated him with such techniques and medicines as were available in that long-ago time but they were of little help and, for all practical purposes, his recovery was due to the good luck that pursued him to the end of his days.

At first the routine of hospital living was pleasant enough. He was weak and sleepy, and the clean bed with its starched sheets was a comfortable haven. But as the months passed, strength and health returned and the soreness ebbed out of his belly; with the change in his health came the first twinges of homesickness.

The yearning to escape, to get back to friends, relatives, and the company of enticing young women, assumed overwhelming dimensions. By the summer of 1919 Lilley was "about to go stir crazy."

One by one the men in the wards slipped away as wounds healed and amputees learned the uses of artificial limbs. Lilley was quartered in a large ward and week by week the unused beds multiplied, their mattresses rolled up and the springs glaring coldly. The banter of friendly voices faded, and for the men who remained life became increasingly lonely. Lilley became obsessed with thoughts of his parents and friends and "the little cool hollers on the Line Fork." He made inquiries about the probable date of his discharge, but the doctors rebuffed him. They made it clear that such a decision was totally within their own province and that a mere private could not fathom the mysteries by which his life was ordered. At last he could stand the boredom no longer and told the medical colonel who visited him occasionally that he wanted to go home, that practically everyone else who had served in the war had long since been released, and that he should be released also. Lilley declared that he could see no improvement brought about by the pills he was swallowing and that "a man would be a heap sight better off at home than here in this old lonesome hospital."

For this outburst he received an icy stare from the colonel but no other reply. The days lengthened into another dreary and changeless fortnight. At last a brilliant idea entered his head and Lilley asked for a one-day pass to go out and see the sights of "Washington City." This modest request was routinely approved, and the homesick youth left the hospital at nine-thirty on a bright clear morning in late summer, with nine hours of freedom before him. A little after eleven he stepped from a streetcar a few blocks from the White House and, resolutely squaring his shoulders, strode briskly toward the gates that provided entrance to the executive mansion from Pennsylvania Avenue. Lilley was about to demonstrate the principle by which he

11

would conduct his entire life: when he wanted something, he went and asked for it.

A marine stood at attention on each side of the massive iron gates but the grim, impassive faces did not deter him. He turned in and undertook to pass between them but, quick as a flash, they stepped in front of him, snapped their Springfields in a brisk "present arms," and completely obstructed his way. One of them, a sergeant, informed Lilley in clipped and certain terms that neither he nor anyone else could enter the White House without specific authorization from the control desk. All visitors must have appointments confirmed in advance. Lilley, of course, had none. He possessed only a pass authorizing him to be absent from his base for nine hours, and almost two of those hours had already slipped away.

Lilley explained his predicament. After all, there had been marines in France and he and they had been comrades in arms. All the rest of his old buddies had long since returned to their homes. All, that is, who had survived the bullets and grenades of Ludendorff's army. On the other hand, Lilley was compelled to sit out tedious days at the hospital, far from home and "lonesome to death." All he wanted was a few words with the president so things could be set straight and he could get home at last. Five or ten minutes would be enough for the purpose.

But the stern faces of the marines remained immobile. The sergeant reiterated, "You can't just walk into the White House, soldier! You have to have a confirmed appointment. Every Tom, Dick, and Harry in the country can't walk in and start up a bull session with the president of the United States!"

Lilley was stumped. Back home in the hills, any public official one needed to reach was easily accessible in the county courthouse. The county and circuit judges, sheriff, tax assessor, and assorted clerks could be accosted at will. When the governor, congressman, or senator came to town on a campaign speaking tour, hundreds of people shook his hand and wished him well. Lilley explained all this to the sergeant. But the noncom shook his head and warned with utter finality, "Move on, soldier, and shut up, or I will call the MPs and they will hustle you to the nearest stockade. Then you will have a mess of trouble on your hands, sure enough!"

During this unavailing dialogue Lilley became aware that a tall, distinguished figure had approached from the direction of the White House and had stopped just behind the two marines. The man was about fifty-five, with strong, leonine features and graying hair. His form was still slender and he was dressed in the most outlandish garb Lilley had ever seen. His trousers were vertically striped gray and black, the shirt snow-white and stiff with starch, and the coat somber black with tails that descended in the rear to a point just behind the knees. Above it all was a tall, stiff black hat, round as a stovepipe and covered with shiny silk. The gentleman listened carefully to all that Lilley said, his penetrating eyes fastened on the Kentuckian's agitated face.

When it was apparent that Lilley could not get into the White House and speak to his commander in chief—that his way was barred and that he wholly lacked the capacity to do anything about this unexpected impediment—new hope was stirred by the soft but commanding voice that came from one Lilley immediately sensed to be a friend. With a courteous but regal nod to the marines the gentleman entered the discussion.

"Sergeant," he said, "please be so kind as to let me have a few words with our friend here. After all he has fought for his country and been wounded in its service, and that entitles him to a hearing at the very least." The marines waited in stoic silence while the newcomer addressed the heartened private from Skyline, Kentucky.

"Soldier," he said, "I have heard a considerable part of your conversation with these marines and I can sympathize with your predicament. On the other hand," and here he beamed at the two guards, "they have a strict duty to perform and, as the sergeant has said, there are rules. A person can't just walk into the White House at any time he wants to do so." Then, with a half-

13

hidden twinkle in his gray eyes, "Now suppose you start all over and tell me your entire story. Just why do you want to talk to President Wilson?"

As Lilley would relate it to me nearly four decades later, he "lit in and told him all about hit, from the day I was mustered in plumb down to that very day thar in front o' the president's house." The gentleman listened without an interruption or question, and when the story was finished, leaned on his polished walnut cane for a minute or more before speaking.

"Private Cornett," he said with immense dignity, "the president is an extremely busy man. More important, he is not an entirely well man. As a matter of fact, I have just come from a conference with President Wilson and I know that he has several hours of work before him. However, I think he will find you and your story of interest if he has time to work you into his schedule. I will be pleased to take you to his office—if, of course, these very able and conscientious marines will permit me to do so—and ask President Wilson to talk to you. He may be unable to see you—I can promise you absolutely nothing in this respect—but we can try, and, after that, everything else is in the hands of the gods."

Lilley was so delighted, so unreservedly grateful that he could say nothing, but he wrung his benefactor's hand with a fervor that bared his soul. Privately, though, he took note of the reference to "the gods," because Lilley had been brought up on the "Old Regular Baptist" doctrine which held that there was one God and no more, with Jesus as his son and the Holy Ghost as his messenger and servant. The strange remark planted some reservations in Lilley's mind but he kept them entirely to himself as, with the consent of the marines, he and his new friend strode up the winding pavement that led amid beds of flowers, huge trees, and neatly trimmed grass to the executive mansion.

As they approached the White House, the gentleman asked Lilley "a sight of questions." He wanted to know Lilley's political affiliation and chuckled a little when he learned that Lilley

14

and practically everybody else who lived along Line Fork Creek was a staunch Republican. He asked the name of the rural post office that served Lilley's community and when told that it was "Skyline" wanted to know who was postmaster and when he was appointed. He asked whether that public servant was well liked by the people and was doing a good job. When Lilley answered that he was the only Democrat in the entire precinct, had been "put in office" by President Wilson and "warn't too well thought of a-tall," his interrogator threw back his head and roared with laughter. Lilley couldn't see the point of the joke, but managed to laugh a little bit himself "just to be on the safe side."

At the entrance Lilley's benefactor was admitted with an easy familiarity that betokened frequent visits. He explained to other guards and to the "head clerks" that his soldier friend wanted to see the president and that he was confident the president would find the soldier and his story extremely interesting. Yes, he knew of the president's tight schedule but they were willing to wait until some time was available. And if it turned out that the president could not see them at all, they would understand and no harm would be done.

Lilley looked around him in wonderment at the huge, carpeted high-ceilinged waiting room. The chairs were upholstered in dark red leather, and provided a dimension of comfort he had never imagined possible. The windows glittered, their light reflected in the rich luster of mahogany wall panels. Typewriters clattered in adjacent rooms and people hustled about with handfuls of important-looking papers. A huge walnut-encased clock slowly ticked off the minutes and as two hours slipped into the abyss of eternity the solemn people with their stiff white shirt-collars and ponderous briefcases disappeared one after the other through the immense doorway beyond which waited the president of the United States. Slowly the magnificent chairs and sofas emptied, and Lilley perceived that when the clock struck one he and his new friend had become the next in line to see

15

Woodrow Wilson. They were alone in the great room except for occasional intrusions by people Lilley would remember as "White House work hands."

During the interval Lilley had responded to a score of questions about life in the hills and his adventures and mishaps in France. He described the old farm not far from the mouth of Defeated Creek where his great-grandfather and a half dozen other hunters had been routed by Choctaws who hid in a canebrake and fired on the white hunters. He told about the one-room log schoolhouse he had attended for five terms, the moonshine still he and his brothers Ed and Jont had operated at intervals at the head of Coon Hollow, and the malt-rich flavor of corn whiskey that trickled from its "worm." Then responding to a new line of questions, he told about the war in France, the ruined forest at Argonne, the thunderous barrages followed by ferocious infantry charges that shattered the enemy lines. He "recollected" the frantic moment when he picked up a long-handled entrenching shovel and pounded the helmeted head of a German corporal down between his shoulders. This had been necessitated, he explained, by the persistent efforts of the German to "job" Lilley with a bayonet. His benefactor had chortled at all these accounts but he became suitably solemn when Lilley described the engagement in which he was wounded and the dreadful misery he had suffered while lying on the battlefield waiting for stretcher bearers. "There I was," he recounted, "shot square through twice, bleedin' like a stuck hog and with the sun bilin' down like a furnace. I was as miserable as a chicken ketched by a big owl."

As this narrative of his battlefield adventures drew to a close, a prim little man with neatly parted hair and carefully trimmed mustache came from beyond the immense doors Lilley had watched so hopefully. Lilley and his friend stood up as the presidential aide drew a thin gold watch from a vest pocket and glanced at the black hands that crept tirelessly around the porcelain dial. His smoothly shaven face crinkled into a beaming smile. "The president has had a good day and has held up well. He has asked me to tell you that he will be pleased to see you."

Then with a friendly tap on Lilley's arm, "He has an especially warm spot in his heart for servicemen, particularly those who have been wounded. Occasionally he doesn't have time for a cabinet member but a soldier, well, that is a different matter." At this little sally he and Lilley's friend laughed as they turned toward the president's office.

As the door clicked shut behind them, Lilley's eyes took in "the quair-shaped room" in which so much of the nation's life had been discussed and shaped by many presidents. Lilley would recall it as being "outlined like a big egg," and at one end near high windows overlooking the spacious grounds stood an immense desk of polished red mahogany. Behind the desk, his face haggard and thin but smiling, sat Woodrow Wilson. The homesick youth from a far-off Kentucky valley trembled a little when he considered the majesty of the man and the place, because from the frail figure in this huge room had come the orders that had sent Lilley and scores of thousands like him against popping Mauser rifles and chattering Maxim machine guns. Here was the commander in chief whom they had obeyed to blood and death, and as the man rose to greet them Lilley suddenly felt good, reassured by a conviction that the people had chosen well. After that Lilley was at ease, all nervousness and tension drained out of him by the president's sincerity and cordiality.

Lilley gripped the hand that was extended to him while his friend handled the introductions with a courtliness and grace that treated the two as equals in every respect. With similar grace and charm the president beckoned Lilley to a seat and requested that he draw it closer to the desk. Lilley looked carefully at the worn, gaunt face and took note that the hand was cold, "almost like a dead fish. I knowed fer shore that death was close fer Woodrow Wilson when I talked to him that day. When a man's a-dyin' hit can't be hid."

The president asked many of the same questions his visitor had already answered. There were inquiries about his home in Kentucky and, to Lilley's surprise, more queries about the postmaster. His forthright responses caused the president and Lilley's friend to exchange smiles and a few chuckles, and once the commander in chief slapped his leg with glee. Lilley would never cease to wonder why they both seemed so interested in the little "one-gallus post office at the mouth of Big Branch."

The president then turned to his military service, his length of time overseas, his battle experience, and his hospitalization. Lilley had no complaints about the war or his training for it, but when the opportunity came he laid his problem precisely where Harry Truman would later say the buck always stops—on the desk of the president of the United States. "Mr. President," he said with the simple dignity of a farmer, "I want to go home. The war's been over for nigh on a year and I need to git back to the Line Fork."

The man who as president of Princeton University had heard many a tale of youthful trouble listened gravely as this homesick lad poured out his woes. The army had been good to him, Lilley asserted, and he had never regretted his part in the war or his painful wounds. He appreciated the medical treatment the army had provided and assured the president that it had been good at all times. "But fer several months now the doctor ain't done a thing fer me. Once in a while I take a few pills and the rest of the time I jist lay around in the ward. The doctors come through in the mornin' and ask how I'm a-doin' and I say 'fine,' and that's all there is to hit. They ain't helpin' me a bit in this world and I want to be discharged. Prac'ly ever'body else has been sent home already, and," with a look directly into the president's calm, level eyes, "I want to go home too. That's why I've come here, Mr. President, to ask you to let me go home."

The president sat in silence for a minute or two, the tips of his fingers pressed together in front of his chest, his ailing form leaning back against the leather of his huge swivel chair. His eyes gazed into Lilley's but so calmly as to give no hint of his reaction to the unusual plea.

At last he spoke and his tone was reassuring. "Doctors," he began, and the slender hands gestured almost helplessly, "are a stubborn lot. They are very hard to order about and I am not

18

sure we should even try. After all, they are experts in human health and we laymen may interfere with their decisions only at great risk to the people physicians are trying to help. We could easily do the wrong thing and a doctor might, as a result, see his patients worsen or even die. So we must be careful. We can take no step detrimental to your health, or that of any other soldier."

He reflected again. "Ultimately your discharge must be based on medical grounds alone. The government owes you treatment as long as it offers hope of continued improvement. You have many years of life ahead of you, and the government must see that you enter those years in the best health we can achieve. That, after all, is exactly what your doctors are trying to do for you. They want you to go home as a well man. Doubtless their examinations reveal to them things you do not suspect. Perhaps you still have a bit of fever, or those two bullets may have injured an organ in some way they have not told you about. They may even plan some corrective surgery. Doctors are a secretive lot who see a lot more than they tell their patients."

He turned his chair and looked out the window at the great trees, and there was a ruefulness about him that went straight to Lilley's heart. The mind and nerve were still strong, but the system that supported them was in decline, and for a moment the three seemed to share an unspoken sorrow that one of them was marked for death at no distant date.

When he turned back to Lilley his whole aspect changed. His face beamed in the smile that had electrified the world. "I can't promise to get your doctors to change their minds, but I can make some inquiries." He tapped the telephone on the corner of his desk, "I will make some calls for you, and I have *some* influence at Walter Reed. Sometimes a call from the president will speed things up and help out a bit," and here he winked at Lilley in a most confidential way.

The president stood up to indicate that the meeting should end. He and Lilley shook hands a second time and the soldier told the author of the Fourteen Points that he was "much obliged" to him for his kindness. The president patted Lilley on the arm and his parting words were, "Don't lose heart and we'll see what comes of our meeting." And then when Lilley was at the door, "It was kind of you to come and see me. Thank you, and good luck!"

On Pennsylvania Avenue, Lilley and his benefactor talked a few moments while they awaited the streetcar that would carry the patient back to his ward. "You made a great impression on the president and brought some relief to work that is often tedious and tiring." He looked at his watch and smiled at the hours flown from his own work schedule. "I don't begrudge a minute since I met you this morning. I share the president's good wishes for your future and hope that you will live for many years and have only the best of luck through all of them." The streetcar arrived with a clanging of bells and Lilley mounted the steps. When he looked back, the gentleman was leaning on his cane and gazing after him. Only then did Lilley realize with a start that he had not learned the name of the man who had treated a lonely private with so much warmth and solicitude.

The next day passed with the old familiar routines. Lilley got up at six-thirty, showered and shaved, and ate breakfast at seven-fifteen. A little past nine his doctor, a lieutenant-colonel, came by, looked at the chart attached to the foot of his bed, asked a few questions concerning Lilley's bowel functions, took a new temperature reading, and departed. When Lilley asked about the possibility of a discharge the only answer was a non-committal shrug. Discouraged somewhat, Lilley swallowed "two little white pills" three times during the day and spent the rest of the time wandering about or lying on his bed staring up at a ceiling he had already studied with infinite attention to every detail.

But if that day was one of idleness and lassitude, the one that followed most assuredly was not. A few minutes past eleven a major strode into the ward with a brusqueness that indicated utmost purposefulness and no little indignation. He walked straight to Lilley's bed and, glaring first at the name card and then at Lilley, observed, "Well, well, well, you are Private Cornett, I see."

Before Lilley could respond to this inanity, the major commanded, "Put on your shoes and ward coat and follow me immediately!" Lilley did as he was told and toiled to keep a pace or two behind the fuming officer, whose step could scarcely have quickened if Satan had been at his heels. Along corridors they went, up in a soaring elevator, and then the length of another corridor to a waiting room outside a door with a neatly lettered brass plate above it bearing the single word "Commandant." Lilley was prepared for the usual tedious wait, but on this day no waiting was in order. The major opened the door, gestured Lilley in after him, and closed the door with a click of ominous finality. Lilley was almost unnerved by the spectacle that met his eyes.

Extending through the center of the room was a long conference table with chairs ranged about it, and in the chairs were a dozen physicians. Lilley saw in a few seconds all the men who had seen him since he had been at Walter Reed—X-ray specialists, his regular ward physicians, and five or six others who had consulted with them in medical mumbo-jumbo at occasional bedside conferences. All were there, all were looking directly at him, and there was not a friendly expression amongst them. At the far end of the table sat a rangy, balding man of about fifty, the single star of a brigadier general glittering on his shoulder straps and collar. He sprang to his feet as if stung by a gigantic hornet and demanded, "What in the God-damned hell do you mean by going to see the president of the United States? Just who in hell do you think you are, anyway?"

Lilley could think of no worthwhile replies, and after a few other outraged and profane comments the general regained a semblance of composure and told Lilley to sit down, indicating a seat considerably removed from the nearest healer. When he had settled himself into the chair, the doctors gazed coldly at him for a minute or more. Lilley saw that each physician had a few

21

sheets of paper before him, the very lined pages on which notations had been made at those bedside conferences.

The general made a new effort to control his wrath at the upstart private. "Soldier, you have done a most unusual thing, to say the least. It is not every day that a buck private walks into the White House and asks the commander in chief for a discharge." After this bolt he glared with renewed malevolence. "I have had a call from the president about you, and because of that call I have convened these doctors. They are thoroughly familiar with your problems and I want you to hear what they have to say, and later today I intend to call the president and summarize their opinions for his information. You may or may not believe it, but every man in this room has your best interests at heart and wants you restored to good health and sent home. And sometimes what seems very clear and simple to the patient is a good deal more difficult and uncertain to his doctor. Now, I am going to ask each of these gentlemen to tell you what he thinks about your situation and whether you should receive further treatment or be discharged."

He then called on a colonel who, as chief of medicine, had reviewed all of Lilley's records and had no hesitation in recommending several additional months of the same medical regimen. The general then questioned the others, in descending order according to rank, until the lowliest captain had been heard from. Referring to his notes, each in turn told Lilley about his examinations, diagnosis, and recommendations. All believed treatment should be continued a while longer, though their reasons for so believing varied. When the last had spoken, a silence prevailed while the general pondered the object of all this unusual activity. Lilley too remained silent. The commandant demanded, "Well, you have heard the opinions of your doctors. You know what the medical staff thinks is in your best interest. In view of what you have heard, what do you want to do?"

Without a moment's hesitation Lilley shot back, "These pills ain't doin' me no more good than so much bug dust, and I want to go home. I want out of the army and the sooner the better! "

The general stood up and the other officers hastily followed suit. To the private the general directed an exceedingly curt dismissal, and without the company of the major Lilley wandered back to his ward. He took a wry pleasure in the fact that he and the president and his nameless benefactor had at least stirred things up a bit.

About the middle of the morning on the following day the major made another businesslike appearance. He demanded that Lilley follow him to a storeroom where supply clerks provided him with a new uniform as graceless and ill-fitting as the one he had put on as a recruit. When he was encased in the scratchy clothing and heavy brown shoes he accompanied the major to an office where various forms were presented to him for his signature. He annoyed the adjutant-general's representative by carefully reading each of the documents before signing it, a process that left the major fidgeting and drumming his fingers against the top of his desk. One set of papers summarized the nature of Lilley's wounds, certain minor illnesses from which he had suffered, and the diagnoses and treatments of various physicians, including the unpronounceable names of medicines he had so patiently ingested. Another document reflected his pay during his two years of service and when it had been signed the major counted out the money then owing, plus sixty dollars as a mustering-out allotment. Then he handed Lilley a voucher redeemable at any United States railroad office for tickets to the station nearest his home. After all these were duly receipted, the major drew a crisp new military discharge out of his desk, the defiant eagle of the United States emblazoned at its top. The officer demanded to know whether all was in order, to which Lilley replied, "I reckon it is. At least I ain't complainin' about any of hit so far." Thus assured, the major uncapped his fountain pen and signed the certificate on behalf of the adjutant-general of the army of the United States. He handed it, too, to Lilley who, with the same attention he had devoted to the other papers, now slowly read it from top to bottom. It attested that the soldier had borne true, faithful and honorable service to the United States, in witness whereof the signature and seal had been affixed.

The major unbent enough to bestow upon Lilley the perfunctory handshake ordained for all new civilians, and the exultant Mr. Cornett dashed back to the ward to collect his meager personal belongings and bid farewell to the nurses, orderlies, and few remaining patients. Shouts of astonishment went up when he burst through the door resplendent in the crinkly new uniform and beaming with satisfaction. He shook hands with the patients, dropped a hint or two to the nurses about his plans for the young ladies back home, and vowed to remember their many kindnesses to him. He dumped his possessions into a small canvas carrying case and started for the door followed by shouts of farewell and good wishes. But before he reached the end of the ward his exuberance was dashed to darkest gloom and misgiving. The major surged through the door afire with mission and purpose. "Ah, there you are!" he said, relief plain in every feature, "I'm glad I caught you before you left the grounds." He held out his hands. "Here, let me have that discharge," he demanded, and in a twinkling had disappeared with Lilley's long-coveted evidence that he was an ex-soldier and free to go home.

Lilley sagged down on the bed he had so recently forsaken, dejection flooding his soul. "Lord have mercy," he thought, "they ain't a-goin' to let me go home after all." All his new schemes began to evaporate amid the raillery of his friends. One yelled, "You're not goin' home till after the next war, Cornett. The girls will all be married and have grandchildren by the time you get back to the farm." He meditated on this possibility for a few moments, his demoralized spirit struggling to devise a fresh plan of escape from the hated hospital.

But his new worry was short-lived. Within a few minutes the major was back and the discharge was restored to Lilley's hands. He took it and unrolled the stiff formal sheet to see what, if anything, had been done to it. To his delight it was unaltered except

24

for a single typewritten sentence across the margin—the same sentence that would catch my eyes many years later: "Discharged by Order of the President," and signed by the brigadier-general as commanding officer of the hospital.

Little Thuggie

THERE was anger in the land in the 1930s. The depression wore on, and large families had to be fed on low wages. Even after the mines were unionized, the improvements that came were mostly of morale. People were more hopeful and conditions seemed better, but food remained scanty, clothing thin and ragged, and dollars few until Pearl Harbor and the war. The people in the mining camps and on eroded hillside farms felt betrayed and victimized.

It was accepted with little cavil that the hard times had been engineered by big business for reasons none could articulate. On commissary porches and in the mines when men stopped to "eat dinner" there was talk that the government ought to take over.

The hero of the coal miner was Franklin D. Roosevelt. He was the workingman's friend, his advocate and protector against the bosses. If FDR had called for nationalization of the coalfields, the men whose labor produced the dusty black lumps would have supported him vociferously and with near unanimity.

Miners had another hero only a notch less esteemed than Roosevelt. He was John Llewellyn Lewis, the towering Welshman-by-way-of-Iowa who had battled to bring the United Mine Workers back from the brink of collapse and had organized the Congress of Industrial Organizations to challenge the cautious American Federation of Labor. His immense, shaggy eyebrows, his Shakespearean thunderbolts hurled at the flinching coal operators, and his flamboyant battlecry "No contract, no work!" endeared "John L." to miners and their families.

In most eastern Kentucky counties unionization came in 1933 or 1934. The operators were weakened past the power to resist by consecutive years with few or no orders for their product. They hoped the NRA with its blue eagle, and wages stabilized through unionization, might stop the relentless deflation and help them start a comeback. They signed the contract and hoped for the best.

But in Harlan County things were different. The giant mine at Lynch was owned by United States Coal and Coke Company, a subsidiary of United States Steel. The parent company was unalterably opposed to the United Mine Workers, the Communist-sponsored National Miners Union, and any and all other labor organizations. It touted the "right of contract" and the fiction that a penniless coal digger living in a four-room company house could negotiate and contract on a equal basis with a company that produced more finished steel in a single year than Germany, Italy, and Japan combined. The lesser operations elsewhere in the county were devoted to the same opinion and vowed never to accept collective bargaining. Unions, they said, were un-American.

D. C. Jones, known as "Baby" Jones, was judge of the circuit court. Kentucky had a law against "criminal syndicalism," and Baby, whose wife was a coal operator's daughter, was determined that syndicalism should never raise its ugly head in Harlan County. The Arm of the Court was Sheriff John Henry Blair, a rabid and fearless labor-baiter and union-hater. He had scores of armed deputies to spy out syndicalism and radicalism, and in a pinch could rely on eight constables and the state highway patrol. But these were not all. The Harlan County Coal Operators employed "industrial policemen" to "protect their property." These, too, were appointed as sheriff's deputies with full power to enforce the law and make sure that miners avoided syndicalism, radicalism, and unionism. U. S. Coal & Coke brought in an offshoot of the Coal and Iron Police—the hard-boiled organization that had terrorized the Pennsylvania fields in an earlier time.

The companies used the blacklist to shut out of employment all who were known to have been union members, who advocated unionism, or who were known to have talked to a union representative. The multitudes of miners were totally dependent on their employers for shelter, and the house contract a man was required to sign before occupying a coal camp house left him at the mercy of the company. The covenant permitted him to stay on the company's property and to occupy its house "at the convenience of the company as the tenant's employer," and required him to move from the house immediately at the company's demand. If men got "out of line" and sought to exercise the right to organize and bargain collectively which New Deal legislation had granted them, they could be ordered out of their homes and compelled to leave the town. In those days the company owned the entire town and a vast district surrounding it. If evacuated they had nowhere to go except to the public road, and there they became "vagrants." Baby Jones abhorred vagrancy, as did the lesser lights of the Harlan County judiciary—the county judge, justices of the peace, and police judges. The eminent circuit judge could scarcely sentence the swarms of vagrants and "syndicalists" to the penitentiary, and the jail could not contain them. So he usually "took pity" on the offenders—after all, they were laboring men with children to feed—and simply ordered them out of the county.

The deputies and the industrial police were everywhere. Companies that scrimped on their taxes so that school teachers were lucky to draw seventy-five dollars a month found abundant funds for "officers" and their automobiles, motorcycles, uniforms, pistols, and submachine guns. There were funds, too, for spies who worked in the mines and listened, who were among miners taking "the obligation" as UMW members, and who infiltrated groups meeting secretly to plan the enlistment of new members. These activities were communicated to company officials, and the inevitable evictions, arrests, and prosecutions followed. The companies referred to the men who enforced their

28

orders and the orders of their judges as peace officers. In their eyes, the officers dutifully protected property, enforced the plain language of contracts, and upheld Americanism.

But to the tormented and embattled coal miners and their families they were gun thugs, detested as spying, treacherous, and ruthless oppressors.

The UMW's struggle to organize Harlan County was epic in scope and duration. It lasted nearly seven years and cost dozens of lives. Eventually Lewis was able to arm his miners and the bloody war was fought out to its conclusion. The miners prevailed because they had already lost everything and had nowhere to go but up. They waged a form of people's warfare against the hated "thugs" and won.

I remember a visit to my uncle, Jim Wyatt, a mild little man I thought to be utterly harmless. Yet he had a new Winchester rifle hidden in a closet, to which he referred with a sly smile as a "John L. Lewis special." There were many such "specials," and other models also.

But the men would never have triumphed without their wives, sisters, and daughters—those hard, embittered, gaunt women who encouraged and sometimes goaded them to persist. In 1970 I heard a story that illustrates the lengths to which at least one woman was willing to go.

When I left the practice of law at the end of 1976, I found particular pride and pleasure in my part in the landmark case of *Blankenship* vs. *United Mine Workers of America*. I was co-counsel with Harry Huge of the Washington firm of Arnold and Porter in that lawsuit which opened the pension fund of the United Mine Workers to thousands of Kentuckians who had fought the brutal battles of the 1930s for "the organization," only to be jettisoned without pension or medical care in their old age. The successful conclusion of the case brought scores of aged men to my office to inquire about their eligibility under the terms of the settlement. From Clover Fork in Harlan County came an old man—wizened, stooped, thin, short of breath, and racked by the dry, persistent cough of "black lung." His still-sturdy wife was with him, and his youngest son, a robust and ruddy soul of thirty-five. The old people were at least seventy.

Matters worked out satisfactorily for him and the retirement pension was approved, together with a considerable lump sum accrued to that date. He and his wife were born in Breathitt County, moving to Lynch in 1923. There he worked in the immense mine of U. S. Coal & Coke, then operating in the superlative Imboden Vein. In those days of hand loading, Lynch had a population of 10,000, and my clients were living there in that new town when the "troubles" came.

My attention was caught by the curious nickname the old woman applied to her son. Two or three times she referred to him as "Little Thuggie." After a while my curiosity got the better of me and I asked for an explanation. "That is an unusual nickname," I said. "Why in the world do you call him 'Little Thuggie'?"

She looked at her husband inquiringly, hesitating to answer without his consent. He coughed in the hard, shallow manner of the silicotic and said, "Go ahead and tell him all about it. I don't care, and besides everybody who would have any interest in it is already dead but me, and I ain't got long to go."

The woman said that in 1933 the company employed a particularly odious thug. He was from Alabama and had a narrowness and a glint about his eyes that showed a willingness to kill at little or no provocation. He was a tall man, with blond hair and a tendency to corpulence. He wore a bluegray uniform consisting of a straight-brimmed trooper's hat, jacket with Sam Browne belt, and riding breeches. His legs were encased in tightly laced high boots that were always immaculately polished. There was a huge pistol at his side. He made his rounds on a motorcycle that carried a "gun-boot" into which was thrust the deadly wood and steel of a .45 caliber Thompson submachine gun.

"That man was poison," she said. He evicted families from their homes with a dispatch and brutality that showed he enjoyed every minute of it. He had pistol-whipped men who hesitated for even a moment when told to move on. He liked to stand at the drift mouth of the mine when men emerged cold, hungry, and tired at the end of the shift, the submachine gun cradled in his arms and an arrogant swagger to his walk. He said he had killed five miners in Alabama and would kill ten in Harlan County before he left. He was hated by the miners.

But the wives of the miners loathed him. His manner was as arrogant and sadistic toward them as toward their husbands. When he found a child playing in an area marked No Trespassing, he applied his jackboot to the urchin. When a spirited woman "sassed" him in front of the enormous stone commissary building, he slapped her face, then taunted her helpless husband. He "was ripe for killing," as the woman in my office said.

One night when her husband prepared for bed she laid down the facts of life to him. "You are never goin' to sleep with me agin till you go kill that thug. If you don't kill him you can forget all about makin' love to me!''

She recalled that her declaration "upset him a sight on earth." He joined in to admit as much. "I sort of hated to go and just flat-out kill him without givin' him a chance."

But his wife said the man didn't deserve a chance. There was a war on, and in a war the object is to kill without being killed. The ambush is the thing, she advised. "Kill the lowdown son-of-a-bitch before he knows what is happenin' to him."

The frail old man at my desk was a lusty thirty-five in those days, and his wife's decision was hard to live with. Still, she was a woman of her word, and he went to work to set things straight again within his conjugal affairs.

He owned a "right good shotgun" which he used for squirrel hunting in the fall. The cartridges he possessed were loaded with small shot, not at all suitable for hunting thugs. He had no automobile, but a "mining buddy" owned a Model A Ford. On a Saturday morning he talked his friend into driving him across the Pine Mountain to Whitesburg in the adjoining county of Letcher. There he bought four Super-X shells loaded with "double-ought

31

buckshot." He didn't want a Harlan County merchant recalling the sale of this unusual ammunition when the inevitable investigations began.

Next came careful study of the thug's habits. He went on a regular schedule, patrolling the town, the mine, and the highway approaches to both. Each night nine o'clock saw his growling motorcycle turn at a "wide place" a third of the way up the Big Black Mountain on the road to Virginia. Sometimes he waited there long enough to smoke a cigarette while his sharp eyes looked for suspicious cars that might contain organizers.

One night the thug came as usual, the engine of his motorcycle roaring a warning of his approach. The headlight gleamed as the vehicle bounced over the uneven surface, slowing to a stop where the shoulder of the road was a dozen feet wide. The rider put one foot on the ground and sat astride the machine. He pulled a cigarette out of his jacket and put it between his lips. His thumb turned the wheel on a lighter and a flame sprang up. The lighter was lifted to the cigarette, illuminating the lines of the cruel face as the cheeks sucked in to inhale. At that moment eight or ten heavy lead slugs tore through his head. The thug died in a millisecond without even hearing the boom of the shotgun. When he struck the ground his head was a ghastly and unrecognizable lump of bloody pulp.

When the miner reached home the lights were out, his family in bed. He had hidden the gun far up in the hollow recesses of a decayed beech tree for recovery at a later time. This was not a night to be seen crossing streets and entering doors with a shotgun in one's hand. As for the three remaining .00 shells, they were stuffed deep down in a leaf-filled sinkhole that had remained undisturbed for centuries on the forested hill. There they doubtless remain today.

The wrinkled grandmother laughed as she confessed. "Nine months from that very night a baby boy was born at our house. His daddy named him Lewis Delano after John L. Lewis and Franklin Delano Roosevelt. He usually signs his name with his initials—L. D."

Her hand reached out in a motherly pat on the arm of her hulking son. He grinned in embarrassment over the revelations concerning his genesis. Her eyes brightened with the love only a mother can feel for the flesh and blood she has borne. "Yes, his daddy calls him 'Lewis D.,' but I nicknamed him 'Little Thuggie.' Most of his friends call him that, but they don't know why."

The Mountain
the Miner
and the Lord

SAM HAWKINS was enormous and coal black, with immense chest and shoulders and broad, work-thickened hands. When he told me this story he was about seventy-five, and time and arthritis had slowed him to an uncertain shuffle. But his eyes were still wonderfully alert, and in their dark depths there glowed immeasurable woe and much wisdom.

It was late November in the bleak depression year of 1932 in the coal town of Fleming, Kentucky. The leaves had long since fallen from the few scrub beeches and oaks on the dark hills, and now gray, gloomy clouds hung near their rocky crests. Cold rain beat relentlessly against the tarpaper roofs and weatherboarded walls of scores of identical houses, and a pall of smoke, grime, and grit from the chimneys blanketed the narrow streets and sidewalks. Elsewhere a few well-to-do people had begun to think of Christmas, but in Fleming—and in countless other Appalachian mining communities—people thought only of survival.

The industrial crisis that had closed mills and factories had brought most mines to a complete shutdown and the others to a two- or three-day work week. Tens of thousands of miners were without jobs. Currency had disappeared as if recalled to the mints, and company scrip—redeemable only at company commissaries—was the medium of exchange. All the banks in the county (and most of those in adjoining counties as well) had folded, taking with them the savings of miners, merchants, and coal operators. The fear that lay in the valleys was more suffocating than the smoke-laden fog.

Sam Hawkins was forty-eight and had one child, Margaret. The girl was nineteen, big-boned and strapping like her father. Sam's wife had died in July after an appendectomy. The doctors in the shabby, hopelessly overcrowded little company hospital had done all they could for her, but in those days before antibiotics there was little chance to save her. Sam was with her at the end and, numb with grief and loss, he had ridden with her body in a company hearse driven by a company undertaker to a company graveyard.

Sadie's last words to Sam had been desperate: "Sam, honey, Margaret won't ever git to go to college! She'll be pore and helpless as we is!"

But Sam had not despaired. In the face of incredible odds he had sent his "little girl" off to Kentucky State College for Negroes at Frankfort when the fall term began in September. When she kissed him good-bye and climbed aboard the train, she carried all her possessions in a cardboard box. Wrapped in a handkerchief in her cheap little purse were fifteen one-dollar bills which Sam had gotten from an accommodating white politician in the county seat. For them Sam had exchanged fifteen dollars in scrip and three days of farm labor.

When Sam and Sadie had come up from Selma, Alabama, to the booming Kentucky coalfield they expected to find little happiness for themselves. In the coal towns blacks were "damn niggers," and occasional lynchings kept black coal diggers cowed and quiescent. But life was far better, even so, than any they had known in Alabama. As long as the boom lasted they ate well and had enough clothes, and the company house was warm, dry, and neatly painted. Their daughter was a delight to both of them and they had vowed to educate her. She would go to college and would some day teach school. She would know how to do things they had never dreamed of for themselves—she would read and write. They nurtured a dream to "make somebody" out of their daughter, to see her and their grandchildren slip beyond the cruel oppression of poverty, insecurity, and endless toil.

Some things were encouraging in this respect. When the coal corporations constructed the new towns in Letcher County they had built houses, stores, streets, hospitals, water systems, and schoolhouses—for white children. Several years passed before classrooms were opened for black children, and then only grade schools were provided, but it was a beginning.

In that time and place a high school education was a luxury many communities could not afford to provide. In the struggle to build secondary schools the black children and their parents were forgotten and a stern state law prohibited integrated classrooms. As Margaret made her way up through the Fleming Colored Graded School her parents watched her progress with a pleasure that was tempered by a growing anxiety. Unless a high school could be built soon, their daughter's education would terminate abruptly in her fourteenth year. Sam commenced working on this problem and, as he phrased it, "The Lord blessed me, he shorely did!"

One summer day Sam rode a train fifteen miles down the river to Whitesburg, the shabby little county seat, and, hat in hand, he entered the office of the county attorney. He believed the official's condescension covered a kindly heart and told him his worries. He asked the lawyer to draft a petition to the fiscal court and board of education. The instrument, as pecked out by the attorney on an ancient Underwood, "humbly and respectfully" requested the building of a high school for "colored students" who had "completed the course of studies required for an eighth grade diploma." Sam left the crumbling brick courthouse apprehensive at the thought of the immense task he had undertaken.

In the next few weeks he collected the signatures of Negroes—or more generally their marks, for few could write. Then, when virtually all blacks in Fleming and other nearby towns had marked the paper, he submitted it to white miners, housewives, merchants, and company officials. Most signed, with sly winks and nods to their fellows, though not a few refused because they did not believe in "educating niggers." Some said bluntly that taxes for white schools were burdensome enough without the extra expense of "nigger schools." But the list of scrawls and X's grew steadily longer.

One day Sam and a black preacher enlisted the aid of another white official, a one-armed former coal miner, and laid their tattered document before the eight tobacco-chewing justices of the peace who made up the fiscal court. Two members insulted them for their pains, but the others were more sympathetic. A year and a half later, the county board of education, the fiscal court, and the school officials for the independent district in the town of Jenkins reached an agreement: a high school would be built in Jenkins and administered as a part of the town's system, but the county would contribute annually to its support. Black children from both school districts would attend it.

When the news came, Sam and Sadie felt a glow of pleasure greater than either would ever know again. Sam believed the Lord had done it and said so to all who mentioned his achievement. But before the first stone was laid in the building's foundation Margaret had brought home her grade school diploma. She would have to repeat her last year's work while the carpenters built her high school and administrators struggled to find, somewhere, a black faculty. It was a foregone conclusion that whites would not teach in such an institution.

Fifteen hundred blacks celebrated the opening of their new citadel of learning with a barbecue and home-brewed beer. The preachers prayed long and fervent prayers of thanksgiving. Sam was lauded as the man "who had a vision," and the white school men patted him on his back and congratulated him. That was on a spring day in 1928 when the world was rosy. Margaret got her high school diploma four years later after the sky had fallen, when most men's hopes were as cold as the slate that towered in vast heaps above the coal camps. She read the ornately inscribed certificate to her beaming mother exactly one month

37

before the white undertaker screwed down the pine coffinlid above Sadie's face.

Now as he trudged along the rain-drenched street in the last light of the dying day Sam sagged beneath a new burden. As he turned and mounted the three wooden steps to his door he carried the only food he possessed: a wedge of cheese and a five-cent box of soda crackers. The fire in the grate had dimmed to a mere handful of glowing coals that responded slowly when he knocked out the ashes and added lumps of fresh fuel.

He drew a letter from his pocket and stared at the lines that ran boldly across the white sheet. Sam could not tell one letter from another, but Amos Bryant, the postmaster, had read the brief note to him, and the disconsolate man still remembered every word. There was no escaping them nor what they portended for his child and for his own worth as a man:

Dear Papa,

I miss you and Mama more than I can ever say. Both of you were always so good to me.

My school work is very good and my grades are fine. I really like school a lot.

It looks like I will have to quit school, though, in a few days. My money is all gone and the little work I get is just enough to buy food. Unless you can manage to send me ten dollars I will have to come back home. It will break my heart but I know it will hurt you far more. Maybe that would be best after all, though, because then I could be of some comfort to you in these sad times.

Your loving daughter,
Margaret

Sam's only money lay on the mantelpiece—fifteen cents in the brass scrip of Elk Horn Coal. It was Thursday night and no work for his section of the mine was posted on the board by the payroll window before Monday. A miner was paid on a piece-work basis—thirty-one cents per ton for drilling, blasting, and

38

loading the coal into cars. The company hired a man to undercut the coal at the face, and the miner did the rest. The miner provided his own tools and smithing and the carbide for his lamp. He had to pay the company for the explosives he used. If he was lucky he would net two dollars in eight to ten hours—two dollars in scrip. And if he didn't like the terms he could bring out his tools and starve. Since there was no alternative, the men hung on to the awful jobs, and miners and company together had settled down into abject ruin. Ten dollars was a fortune wholly beyond Sam's reach. He could not borrow, because there was no one with money to lend, and if someone possessed a bit of cash, would he be so improvident as to lend it to a penniless black coal miner? Sam groaned in despair.

The droning rain sluiced against the windows and wooden walls. The wind whirled soot down the chimney and howled about the eaves. Suddenly a new sound emerged from the turbulent night as heavy feet walked across the porch. Knuckles rapped against the door and when Sam, glad to have any visitor, yelled, "Come in," the door swung back to admit a blue-uniformed company policeman.

The spectacle of the officer, his raincoat dripping puddles on the pine floor, sent a new wave of dread along Sam's spine. He had violated no statutes, but a few days earlier he had talked to a representative of the United Mine Workers of America about the possibility of organizing a local. Company spies were everywhere and such "ingratitude" was cause enough to evict an offending miner from company property. And where could a man go on such a night as this?

The policeman looked about the room with its simple furniture, the framed snapshot of Sadie, and the crochet work with which she had tried to bring some beauty to the graceless place. He licked his lips and stared at Sam with pale, uncertain eyes.

"Sam," he said, "the superintendent asked me to stop and tell you that he has a chance for you to make some real money. Yes, some *real* good money! One of the sections has mined out too much coal and a big pillar is taking weight. The men in that section are afraid of a general roof fall, and they won't go into the place. The super says you are the best coal loader in the camp, and you can work all night if you want to. The weight is pushing the coal out from the pillar, and you won't have to do a thing but shovel. A man can load an awful lot of coal between now and daylight." He paused, then added, "The engineers say they are pretty sure the top will hold for another twenty-four hours or longer and, anyway, an experienced miner like you, Sam, can generally tell when the fall is coming in time to get out to a safe place."

To the policeman's amazement the black giant rolled his eyes heavenward and with utter sincerity murmured, "Thank ye, Lord!"

Sam put on his work clothes—long cotton underwear, faded bib overalls, blue denim shirt and jacket, knee-high rubber boots, and a soft miner's cap with a carbide lamp attached to the front. He pumped a half gallon of fresh water into the bottom section of his aluminum dinner bucket and dropped the bit of cheese and handful of crackers onto the food tray.

A few moments later he reached the office of the mine super-intendent. The superintendent leaned back in a creaking oak swivel chair and explained how a foreman had permitted a little too much coal to be removed in Section 4-B Right. "A squeeze is coming, Sam, and the whole territory is going to be lost in a day or two. There is a lot of fine Elkhorn No. 3 there, and if we don't get it tonight we never will, because the whole mountain is going to set down on it." He cleared his throat. "The track is laid up to the face of the coal. It will squeeze out as fast as you can load it and push it away. We can set all the cars for you that you can possibly load. There is no night shift, but we will leave the fan running, and there is no reason why you can't work all night in there by yourself."

He toyed with a paper clip and tapped Section 4-B Right on the mine map that lay before him. "We will pay you thirty-one cents a ton and that is straight pay. No deductions for anything. You'll not need to do any blasting and the only tool you'll need

40

is a shovel. There is a man-car waiting at the drift mouth to take you to the face."

Sam left the warm room and strode through the icy drizzle a hundred and fifty yards to the drift mouth—a huge, arched hole framed with concrete where steel rails reflected the glaring rays of a battery of electric bulbs as they curved into the black shaft. As Sam approached the opening, water rushed in torrents down the denuded slopes, and the tortured mountain, hard-pressed from within and without, loomed immense and terrifying. Just inside the tunnel Sam climbed into an empty car and slouched low against the wooden side. Propelled by an electric locomotive the car hurtled along the heading. Every six feet black locust timbers held up a sawed eight-by-eight white oak "collar" to secure the roof. Two miles from the portal the little train slowed and turned sharply to the right, then sped along for a couple of minutes longer. After another turn to the right it whined to a halt and Sam straightened up to look along the shaft of light from the locomotive that poked like a yellow finger into the darkness.

Where the track turned off into the working place, a long line of empty cars waited on their rusty steel wheels, each loading about 4,000 pounds when filled and "rounded over." From them the rails stretched to the face of the "pillar," a huge rectangle of glittering coal forty feet wide and at least eight feet thick. The seam rose from the smooth slate floor straight up seven feet to the sandstone roof. About its base lay a two-foot ruffle of loose coal, and as Sam filled his lamp with a fresh charge of carbide and turned up the flame to its utmost the roof creaked and groaned and new lumps pushed outward onto the floor. Here and there small slabs of slate had splintered upward out of the floor under pressure from the descending shaft of coal. He lifted out his dinner bucket and set it and his pick against the "rib" or wall a dozen yards back. He put his shovel in an "empty" and pushed the car to a spot within easy shoveling distance. Then the motorman said, "So long, Sam, and good luck," and sent the locomotive careening down the track.

Sam set three white oak props before he began shoveling,

41

driving hickory cap wedges across the top of each of the eight-inch timbers until it was tightly seated. Ten times as much oak would not protect him from the sandstone ledge that sagged above his head, but the props would serve as barometers by which he could gauge the mounting pressure. As the coal pillar yielded, the oak would splinter and shred, crying in protest until it broke.

He picked up the shovel and with a fervent "Be with me, Lord" pushed it along the slate until the broad scoop was filled, then lifted it and dropped sixteen pounds of Elk Horn No. 3 coal onto the wooden bottom of the car. The clatter sent echoes reverberating along the dark shafts and brought a faint whisper of the original sound back to him a few seconds later. Rhythmically, steadily, the shovel rose and fell, the black heap rising moment by moment until it lay glittering and uniform along the entire length of the seven-foot car. Despite the cool clamminess of the air the ventilation fan pushed in to him, Sam's forehead beaded with sweat and when he dropped the shovel to push the loaded car onto the side track he laid aside his jacket. He pulled a brass disk from his pocket and hung it on the "check horn" at the front of the car. The "check" was marked with his number, 67, and would tell the weighman at the tipple that Sam Hawkins had loaded the coal. The workmen had no "check-weighman" at the scale house and Sam could only pray for honest weights. He put his shoulder against another empty and brought it to the face. When he picked up the shovel, the coal he had carried away had already been replaced by new lumps from the breaking face.

For hours the shovel ascended and descended, interrupted only by forays for new cars. After a while Sam lost all track of the number he had loaded. Sometimes he put fresh carbide in his lamp or paused for a drink of water from his bucket. He commenced work at a quarter past eight, and four and a half hours later his pocket watch told him it was time to eat the cheese and crackers. The morsels were gone in a half-dozen bites, and after resting his arms and back for a few minutes, he returned to the coal. This was no night for ease. The words of his girl's letter as brought to him by the droning voice of the postmaster sounded endlessly in his ears, restoring strength to arms that began to ache with fatigue. Once as he pushed an empty into position he wiped the sweat from his face with a gritty hand and murmured, "We goin' to do it, Sadie! We goin' to do it after all!"

A little after five Sam heard the rattle of the man-trip in the main tunnel, followed by the lights and voices of approaching miners. The day's work in 4-C Right was about to begin, and Sam, after laying the last lump on another car, straightened his back and leaned against his shovel. His legs, arms, and shoulders throbbed with great weariness, and his belly rumbled with hunger. His water bucket was empty and his sweat-soaked clothing clung to his gritty flesh. As he stared at the bobbing lamps he trembled and his head sagged against his chest, but the presence of other creatures after the loneliness of the night was wonderfully welcome. Words of greeting gathered in his throat but died unspoken. Suddenly the lights stopped as the men gazed thunderstruck with astonishment at him and his long line of loaded cars. A derisive laugh came from a lanky white man in front as he squatted on his haunches sixty feet away at the entrance to the short tunnel that led to Sam's doomed pillar.

"You crazy nigger," he called, "don't you know you're goin' to git mashed flat as a bean bug in there? The reg'lar shift quit that whole place yisterd'y and the comp'ny pulled out all its equipment!" Laughter rich with scorn tittered along the line of lights. Then as the men shuffled away over the uneven floor one of them muttered, "Man alive, that nigger shore does love to load coal!"

When they were gone Sam looked for the hundredth time at the props. Long ago the bark had loosened and long splinters stood out from the wood. He laid a palm against one of them and felt it vibrate like a tightened banjo string. Suddenly with a low hum a long filament the thickness of a match detached itself from the surface and hung by splinters from roof to floor. A bushel of coal rolled out to his shoe and a slate shard reared up like a tiny soldier out of the tortured floor. "It's time to quit,"

Sam muttered as he carried his dinner pail, jacket, and shovel into the safety of the tunnel. He leaned his shoulders against the "coal rib" for a brief rest before walking to the main tunnel for a ride to the outside.

But Sam's work-stiffened joints were not soon to enjoy the rest they had earned. As he whispered a good southern-style prayer of gratitude that the perilous night was safely past, a new light approached and the voice of Henry Johnson, a mine foreman, inquired solicitously, "Is that you, Sam? I sure am glad to see you safe and sound." He whistled with incredulity, "God damn! Did you load all these cars by yourself?"

Sam emitted a hoarse croak. "Well, me and the Lord together," he replied. "He held up the top."

The foreman counted the cars, seventeen of them, and then came back to stand before the miner. After a moment of reflection he walked down to the end of the track where Sam had toiled the night away. He held his lamp in his hand to inspect the props and pecked with a pick handle against the roof. It sounded solid, but grains of sand from the "working" top dusted downward against his upturned face. He whistled again, this time reflectively.

"Sam," he opined, "you did all right for yourself last night. You made some money and I know you need it. You're a good worker and you don't scare easy. This top is coming, no doubt about it, but not for a while, in my opinion." He put a chew of tobacco between his teeth, chewed, and spat out ambeer. Then, in confidential tones, "Sam, what about another shift? If you feel up to it, I can send your dinner bucket out to the commissary and get it filled and have some more empties shoved in here and you can shovel all day. The superintendent sure will appreciate it if you decide to do it, but after all, you know the danger and you must use your own best judgment about it."

Sam drew in a long breath and let it out slowly. He thought of his weariness, of the shredding timbers, and of the popping sandstone. Then he thought of Sadie and Margaret, and rose to his feet. "Git me some grub and some empty cars," he said, as he picked up his shovel.

The day passed with infinite slowness. The clerk at the commissary who packed his dinner bucket was generous, but Sam did not linger long over his food. Yearning for some hot coffee, he washed his meal down with a long draught of fresh water. He prudently saved back half the food for "dinner time" about eleven. If all went well—and the top held—he should see daylight again by four o'clock that afternoon.

The food brought a flow of new strength, and for a couple of hours the shovel worked at its old tempo. But gradually the muscular arms and legs turned clumsy and heavy. The pain of weariness advanced in him until it gripped him like a gray blanket from crown to toe. As the hours dragged by, a longing for sleep crept into every nerve and sinew, and the cars filled at an ever slower rate. He struggled to stay alert to the danger above his head—the danger that relentlessly reduced the props to columns of splinters and sent cupfuls of sand sluicing across the undiminished heap of coal at his feet.

When he heard the miners returning from 4-C Right, he laid his shovel on top of the last car and strained with all his remaining strength to send it along the tracks. As it gathered momentum a red haze swam before his eyes and he staggered to keep up as the car rolled down the tunnel. Forty yards away he put on his jacket and drank the last of his water. He sat down and pushed his back against a coal car. "I'll rest jist a minute or two before headin' for the outside," he thought as he closed his eyes.

Sam dozed but his sleep was ended by a roar of cataclysmic proportions, an ocean of rending, crashing sound that hurled him down the tunnel like a puppet. The thick layer of sandstone had broken in the mined-out area behind the pillar and, crushing the pillar like a squeezed plum, sent a giant wave of coal rolling before it. From floor to roof the shaft filled with the tumbling lumps. Behind an impenetrable cloud of gritty dust the avalanche finally halted twenty feet inside the tunnel, while the fall echoed

45

and reechoed like dying thunder to the farthest corners of the mine.

When he left the man-trip and walked around the path to the bathhouse he blinked at the sun which was clipping the top of a western ridge. After twenty hours in the recesses of 4-B Right, the pale glinting rays brought tears to his reddened eyes.

When soap and water had washed away the dirt and sweat and eased some of the misery from his flesh, he put on clean garments and went to the commissary. The babble of voices in the showers and later at the food counters came to him as if from a great distance and he scarcely heard the friendly raillery of the miners. Sam was too tired to think of anything but sleep tonight and the mailing of a money order to his girl tomorrow.

He carried home a small bag of groceries and sat by the fire for a long time with a cup of hot coffee in his hand. The heat soothed him and as he relaxed he felt better than he had for months. He fried potatoes and bacon for his supper and "at the edge of dark" went to bed. As he pulled up the patchwork quilt Sadie had made especially to cover his huge frame he murmured again, as he had the night before, "Thank ye, Lord!"

When the payroll window opened the next morning Sam was there to claim his wages. The paymaster called the scale house to check the weights of the cars and as he talked made penciled notes on a pad. When he left the phone, he went into the commissary to determine how much Sam owed the company store. He came back and smiled at Sam through the steel latticework. "Sam, you're in good shape. A few more breaks like night before last and you could afford to quit." He extended the note pad so the miner could see the totally unintelligible markings and, with the point of his pencil moving down the column, continued, "You loaded twenty-eight cars, averaging a little over two tons each, for a total of fifty-eight and a quarter tons. That comes to $18.06. But you owe the store a little and that will have to be deducted." He named a few trifling purchases, including $.23 for Sam's lunch on the day before. "Your store debt is $3.98, and that leaves you a balance due of $14.08."

Sam let out his breath with deep satisfaction. That was more money than he had possessed in many months and Margaret was saved, for the moment at least. But suddenly his eyes widened with chagrin as the paymaster's hand deposited his earnings on the worn board—a fistful of brass scrip.

His strength drained away and a groan escaped him. "Ah no, no sir, not scrip! Not this time! The policeman say 'real money,' and this time scrip won't do. It jist won't do!" And he pushed the brass tokens back through the window. "If I don't git real U.S. money my little girl will jist have to quit school and I can't stand that, no sir!" and Sam, who had not quailed before the sinking mountain, now sobbed aloud.

The paymaster frowned. "You know we've got no money to pay out wages," he snapped. "Scrip is the best the company can do." Then he softened and added, "I'm sorry, Sam. I really am."

Sam stood in the pale autumn sunlight stunned and helpless, his tongue following his broad lips. But before utter ruin enveloped him, he was rescued—at least after a fashion. Another white man, "Mr. Tom" Haymond, the general manager, strode out of his office and approached the window. He asked the paymaster what the trouble was and listened to his explanation and to Sam's renewed plea for cash. He reflected for a long moment, his eyes going from the scrip to Sam's face and back again to the brass tokens. At last he nodded toward the door and said, "Let him in." Sam followed the "big boss" into his office and took the chair Haymond indicated. They stared at one another in silence for a long moment.

"Sam," the executive began, "the company is grateful to you for what you did, but the company is practically broke, and that is the truth." He looked at the ceiling. "We have no money for anything except the most urgent mortgage debts. But I know you love that girl and I honor you for it." Another pause ensued. "I'll tell you what we'll do, if it's agreeable to you. If you can see your way clear to discount your wages from $14.08 in scrip to $11.00 in cash I'll pay it out of the little that's left in our emergency fund."

Sam sprang up and grasped the big boss's hand in whole-hearted confirmation of the deal. Haymond turned the dials on the door of a safe and drew out of a slender envelope two greenbacks—a ten and a one. A few moments later Amos Bryant sold Sam a money order in the sum of ten dollars payable to Miss Margaret Hawkins. The postmaster sold him a stamped envelope for five cents and addressed it as Sam directed. When the envelope with its precious contents fell into the mail slot Sam walked out with sixty-five cents in his pocket.

The day warmed and was sunny and pleasant. Sam felt good again, and hopeful. And for a time things improved generally and he was almost happy.

A little more work became available and, with the passing months and the coming of the New Deal, wages rose somewhat. The miners organized a local union and working conditions improved. Sam was able to send Margaret money from time to time and the girl found a job that provided a little cash in addition to her food. Haymond and the superintendent favored Sam with extra work now and then. Both congratulated him when Margaret came home with her bachelor's degree in the spring of 1936.

She stayed with her father for a year and taught English at the black high school. Then night crashed down as black as coal dust. In the summer of 1937 she was stricken with meningitis and died in the same hospital where Sadie had told Sam good-bye.

Sam did not die with his daughter, nor did he wholly survive her death. He came and went and worked, a figure of immense dignity and integrity, a staunch figure in his church. But he lived the rest of his days with a grief he could not shed, and the old flame of aspiration was never rekindled.

With the years the thick seam of coal in the ridges about Fleming played out, as did Sam and a whole generation of miners. More than a decade has passed since he was buried in the little cemetery next to Sadie and Margaret, and the ancient coal-camp house where he lived so many lonely years now stands silent and empty. The desegregation decision of the Supreme Court closed the doors of the school he worked to build, and vandals reduced it to a shattered wreck. Sam had put little white markers at the graves of his wife and daughter but no one ever got around to marking his own. Perhaps a coal shovel thrust in the earth like a bayoneted rifle over the bones of a fallen hero would be appropriate for such a man.

Christmas Comes to Lord Calvert

CLEON K. CALVERT was a man of strong opinions forthrightly expressed. He was also a fine lawyer with a commanding courtroom presence and much eloquence. He practiced his profession in the Kentucky hills for fifty years and was well known in the courthouses of at least a dozen counties.

He was sometimes referred to as "Lord Calvert," a friendly nickname applied by other lawyers because of the costly brand of whiskey he was reputed to imbibe. Once when he was serving as special judge of the Harlan Circuit Court he partook too freely, a fact that became apparent to spectators in the courtroom. When court was called to order the next morning the judge humbly apologized for his miscreant conduct, found himself guilty thereof, imposed a fine as punishment, and paid the money to the clerk.

For many years Calvert was an attorney for Ford Motor Company. When Ford began buying huge tracts of coal in Harlan, Leslie, and Letcher counties, he supervised the tedious task of abstracting the titles. After this work was completed he maintained a general practice until his death in 1970. He was one of those richly colorful personalities whose extreme individualism once brought renown to the Central Appalachians.

In 1955 I was involved in a lawsuit for title to a tract of coal land. Calvert was my co-counsel and we met to write a brief for the Court of Appeals. He and I and a stenographer spent an entire day at the task and about four o'clock the stenographer left with a twenty-page, triple-spaced, hideously interlined, much corrected and recorrected "rough draft," such as no one but an experienced legal secretary can ever decipher. When she was gone, Calvert asked for a glass of water. He drew a pint of bourbon out of his briefcase, relaxed with sips of Kentucky's most famous product, and told me the following story.

After he relinquished his ample salary from Ford Motor Company, Calvert had cause to regret his decision. When he decided to enter general practice the coal mines were booming, and there were thousands of miners. The glow of prosperity warmed the land. There were innumerable cases for the lawyers—homicides spawned by Saturday night sprees, workmen's compensation claims for injured miners and the widows of the uncountable dead ones, and no end of Prohibition violations.

But the depression came early to the coalfields of southern Kentucky. Mines had multiplied past belief after 1910. By the mid-1920s there was a glut of the fuel in the southern and western states, and postwar economic troubles in Europe had shrunk the demand for export shipments. The boom ebbed away. The ranks of clients in the waiting rooms of lawyers were thinned, and many of those who continued to come were destitute. These unfortunates still needed lawyers as much as ever but could pay little or nothing for their services.

Conditions had gotten pretty tight at the Calvert home when Christmas approached in 1928. Legal fees had become discouragingly few and meager, and the pinch was being felt at all levels. The house needed paint, and all could have used some new clothes. Food was ample but tended to the inexpensive and ordinary. Payments were being met, but just barely, and the bank account was empty. Calvert viewed the future with apprehension.

Judge A. M. J. Cochran had scheduled a two-week session of the United States District Court to be held at London, Kentucky, beginning in mid-December. Hope springs even when the future appears most grim, so with a dubious heart Calvert resolved to attend the term. Perhaps some of the myriad defendants would have both money and the good sense to hire him as their attorney. Even a couple of hundred dollars would be immensely helpful. He would wager the certain expense of a hotel room against the uncertain possibility of fee-paying clients.

The little town of London was a drab place in those days. The farms that surrounded it were worn out and joined their poverty to the destitution of the highland coalfields that converged upon it. He found the federal courthouse jammed with a swarm of lanky, overalled men and goodly numbers of skinny, jaded women. Nearly all were charged with making or selling corn whiskey, or possessing it for the purpose of sale, or transporting the stuff, or sheltering other persons thus offending. Nearly all were guilty as charged but, with few exceptions, claimed to be innocent or offered heart-rending circumstances in extenuation. The most common pleas were poverty (being "up agin it, fer shore"), and having a large brood of children who would starve to death if either parent was locked up. They had profuse excuses, alibis, and justifications, but, alas, they had no money. One offered the counselor ten gallons of good whiskey—"made with water from the drip of the house and so good you can taste the malt real sweet and strong"—while another proffered a "right young milk cow and a suckin' calf" in return for his services, but none had cash.

After four days in which he collected little more than his expenses, Calvert returned to the courtroom on Friday morning. When court convened, the marshal brought in a slender youth whose wrists were handcuffed and fastened by a short chain to a broad leather belt that encircled his waist. Calvert was impressed by the young man's calm, self-assured bearing which was diminished by neither the heavy restraints nor the gazing of spectators. The young man was not more than twenty-two, about six feet tall, handsome and erect. His hair was brown and, though beginning to need a trim, was neatly combed. His features were striking and he glanced at Mr. Calvert with the bluest and frankest eyes the lawyer had ever encountered. Before the youth said a word Calvert was convinced that he was not guilty, that the

52

government was absolutely wrong in the charge it had brought against him.

The indictment was read and Calvert's faith wavered somewhat. It appeared that a couple of weeks earlier federal agents had stopped a truck coming out of Tennessee through Cumberland Gap. It was loaded with whiskey, and the defendant was driving. The truck bore an Illinois license and no one else was in it. The indictment charged him with two counts: possessing an alcoholic beverage in violation of the Volstead Act, and transporting same for the unlawful purpose of selling it.

When Judge Cochran asked him whether he was represented by an attorney, he answered that he was not. Asked (in those far-off pre-Miranda days) whether he was ready to plead to the charge, he said that he was. When the Court inquired whether his plea was "guilty" or "not guilty," Calvert leaned forward to observe his face and hear his answer. The defendant looked at the aged judge and in a clear, ringing voice replied, "Not guilty, Your Honor."

Coming in this straightforward manner, the declaration of innocence left His Honor quite obviously disconcerted. He looked at the defendant for a long moment, doubtless pondering the overwhelming character of the prosecution's evidence, but determined that the presumption of innocence would be fully protected. When he spoke again his tone had softened somewhat.

"You say," began the judge, "that you have no attorney at this time. That being so, do you have the financial capacity to retain an attorney to defend you in this case?"

The answer was as distinct as before. "No, Your Honor, I am sorry to say that I have no money."

Judge Cochran inquired whether he had relatives or friends who were interested in assisting him. Again the reply was negative.

It was the duty of the Court under these circumstances to enter an order designating an attorney to serve as the defendant's counsel. Under the law the attorney would be required to work without pay. Every lawyer with appreciable trial experience had assumed such uncompensated duties dozens of times, and few ever grumbled at the burden such trials imposed upon them. (In the January 1949 term of Letcher Circuit Court—my first term as an attorney—I defended three alleged murderers under such court appointments.) Still, it would be an inconvenience for the lawyer who would doubtless have other things in mind for the day. To go to trial with court-appointed counsel was an indignity a defendant had to cope with throughout the proceedings, and suddenly this was an affront Calvert did not want this youth to bear. Then, too, Cleon K. Calvert had a combative, irrepressible nature and suddenly he felt the distinct need for a hard-fought courtroom battle. Such a struggle would help him cast off his depression, and anyway, the boy said he was innocent and, by God, he might be telling the truth! He certainly looked like he was telling the truth.

Calvert had a son of his own, and who could tell what dark moments might lurk in his future? He might stand before a judge some day, innocent of the charge against him but doomed to suffer because he lacked money to employ a lawyer. Christmas was only a few days away, and red and blue lights had begun to gleam through wintry dusks. Carols were already being hummed by children who whispered about hoped-for gifts. A softer spirit was felt in the land, a sense of brotherliness and charity. It was a season for doing one's best for other people. A good son of the Covenant, Calvert believed in the New Promise. Hard times had strapped him this year so that he could do little for his own wife and child, but he could do something for this unknown, friendless, chained, and penniless young man! He stood up, cleared his throat, and addressed the Court.

"May it please the Court, Your Honor! I understand that this defendant has no attorney and no funds with which to retain one. In order to save the Court the necessity of appointing a lawyer to defend him, I now offer to do so to the best of my ability and without any charge. This is, of course, contingent upon my services being acceptable to the defendant and conformable to the desires of the Court."

Calvert's eyes met those of the defendant for a long moment. He remained standing while Judge Cochran expressed the gratitude of the bench for this commendable proposal. The judge then explained to the youth that the gentleman who had just addressed the Court was Mr. Cleon K. Calvert, an experienced, able, and ethical lawyer. The Court suggested that his offer of free legal services be accepted and inquired whether the defendant had any objection to the arrangement. The reply was, "I have no objections at all, Your Honor, and I am grateful to Mr. Calvert for his kindness."

The Court again commended the attorney for his lofty action—an action, he said, that demonstrated a high regard for Justice and its handmaid, the Law. The clerk entered a minute reflecting Mr. Calvert's offer, the defendant's acceptance, and the Court's approval. Thereupon court was recessed for an hour to allow counsel an opportunity to discuss the case with his new client and to make such other inquiries as he might think proper.

In the conference room the attorney again sized up his client from head to foot. He was impressed anew by the young man he had so impetuously undertaken to save from the federal penitentiary at Atlanta. As he phrased it to me thirty years later, "Innocence just oozed out of that boy!" He learned the defendant's name from his own lips. From that source the good Irish cognomen sounded much less suspect than when read by the clerk and hedged about by the harsh, labored language of the indictment. After a few questions calculated to put his client at ease he asked him to start at the beginning and relate all the circumstances that had brought him to his present hard plight.

In quiet tones and without a single dubious flicker of an eyelash, the young man told his story. He was an orphan. His father had died ten years earlier when the defendant was twelve years old. There had been another child of two at the time, and his mother was pregnant. This situation left the mother with three infants, and in those days before Social Security and Public Assistance, she faced starvation. She moved her brood to a two-room, cold-water flat in one of Chicago's seediest districts. She worked as a seamstress from dawn to dusk but could earn the scantiest subsistence. Her oldest son worked at such odd jobs as he could find, and his dimes and quarters went into the family till. At seventeen he left school to work full time, and for a year or two the family had a much easier life. Then the factory where he worked closed down and jobs became scarce. He went back to part-time and occasional employment, and his mother and brothers suffered real want. To make things worse, his mother became ill and had to spend much time in a charity hospital. This had caused him to assume almost total responsibility for the family. Then one day something totally unexpected happened— something that gave him real hope for a time.

He had been pounding the pavement in search of a job when he dropped in at McGinty's poolroom to escape from the biting autumn wind. He had no money for a game but watched others for a few moments before resuming his quest. As he started to leave, one of the other spectators touched him on the arm and asked whether he could have a few words with him. They went aside to a corner and there he heard a most unusual proposition.

The man was about forty, dressed in a sporty blue suit with an expensive white shirt and silk necktie. A diamond stickpin gleamed in the knot of the cravat. He had learned our hero's name from someone else in the poolroom, but did not identify himself. Names are unimportant, he said, in an honest transaction. And, on being expressly asked, he unequivocally declared the deal to be an honest one, "legal and aboveboard in every way."

This is what he wanted done. On the morning of the next day a van-type truck of a certain description would be parked in a nearby alley. His new and needy young friend would go there by 5 A.M. He would find the cab unlocked, the ignition key under the rubber floor mat. Enough money would be there to pay for gasoline and other expenses, and a road map marked with the routes to be followed. The truck would be driven southward across Indiana and Kentucky, through Cumberland Gap to the little town of La Follette in the hills of Tennessee. It would be

56

parked across the street from the town's only hotel, with the keys left under the floor mat. The night would be spent at the hotel, and on the following morning, after a good breakfast in the hotel's dining room, the driver would return to the truck, retrieve the keys from precisely the same place, and, following the same route, would return the vehicle to the spot in the Chicago alley. He would leave the keys under the mat and go home. On the following day at noon he would return to the poolroom. There he would be handed $300.

It was all simple and easy, honest and lawful. He was being given the chance to earn the money because of those orphaned brothers and their ailing mother. The proposal ended with a friendly nudge in the ribs and, "Because it is getting close to Christmas, I wouldn't be surprised if there happens to be an extry fifty as a bonus."

The recipient of this unusual proposition hesitated. It was all very odd and yet, on the face of it, he would be doing nothing to break the law. He possessed a driver's license and had operated similar trucks. He could make the trip without difficulty. He could not be suspected of stealing the truck because he would return it to the same place. Still, it was dubious, no doubt about it. But there, again, were his sick mother and those two ragged brothers for whom Christmas held no promise. Three hundred dollars would pay old bills and buy new presents. "I will do it!" he said.

The next morning he was at the alley at precisely five o'clock. The truck was at the appointed place and all proceeded according to the plan and the carefully marked road map. He drove all day with only a couple of brief stops, traversing a bit of Illinois, most of the length of Indiana, the rolling Kentucky Bluegrass country, then the rugged hills north of Cumberland Gap. The truck was in excellent condition and slid through "the Gap" an hour after darkness had blanketed the wild ridges. At eleven o'clock the truck was cooling its engine opposite the little hotel, and he was a registered guest inside. He had traveled 650 miles and was numb with fatigue. A late snack was followed by nearly

57

six hours of sleep—the peaceful sleep of the physically weary and spiritually restored.

Before dawn he was on his way north. This time, though, there was a difference. The padlock that held the rear doors was still securely in place, but the truck was no longer empty. While he had slept, someone had filled the van with a considerable cargo. It made no sound when he pulled the truck onto the empty street, but the weight was there, more than a ton of it. He could not see inside and he could not imagine what he was hauling. Consoled by the assurance that all was on the up-and-up, he pushed the gears into high and sped toward the historic gap he had read about in his grade school history books.

A mile inside the Kentucky border he rounded a curve to see a road-block stretched across the highway. There were three cars and several armed men. One of them carried a submachine gun and two others held Winchester rifles. He braked the truck to a halt and his troubles began. The men were federal officers with a search warrant for his mysterious vehicle. A roadside search followed the breaking of the lock, and his astonished eyes beheld stacks of cardboard boxes. An agile agent jumped inside, tore open a carton, and lifted out a tightly sealed quart fruit jar. When the top was twisted off, he smelled for the first time in his life the pungent odor of southern moonshine whiskey. A count revealed that each carton contained a dozen jars, and there were forty cartons.

"I've been in jail ever since, Mr. Calvert. So far as knowing what was in the truck, I am as innocent as the judge." Then with a shrug, "But I guess no one will believe me if I swear it for a hundred years."

Calvert heard the tale with incredulity and astonishment. He wanted desperately to believe the prepossessing youth, and yet it was so preposterous, so fantastic. Would hard-eyed jurors ever swallow such a yarn? Probably not, but then Christmas was near and strange things happen at that gentle season. His fighting spirit flared. "Let's go tell it to the jury," he thundered.

The trial was brief, lasting only a few hours. A jury consisting

58

of a couple of coal operators, a merchant from Harlan County, three or four miners, and a half-dozen hill farmers were interrogated, accepted by both prosecution and defense, and sworn by the clerk to "try the case and a true verdict render." The government called as its first witness an agent who described mammoth bootlegging operations in Chicago and told how the source of the whiskey had been traced patiently back to the Tennessee hills. An informant had telephoned to say that the truck had arrived, and he had worked all night to organize the road-block and obtain the search warrant. Another agent told about the stopping of the truck, the breaking of the lock, the finding of nearly 500 quarts of whiskey. He handed up a jar of the stuff, took off the lid, and passed it around so the jurors could sniff it. Calvert noticed that one or two of them practically drooled as the forbidden liquid was handed back to the officer. The witness pointed his finger at the defendant and identified him as the driver of the truck and its sole occupant. The road map, marked with red ink along routes to be followed, was studied by the jurors. The prosecution rested its case and the triumphant district attorney looked at defense counsel with an air that said, "Come on, Calvert! Quit kidding yourself and give up. You can't squirm out of this one!"

Calvert disdained to make an opening statement and immediately beckoned his client to the witness stand. He did not disappoint his attorney. The manacles had been removed for the trial, and he stood as straight as a soldier, his hand raised at a right angle to take the oath required of a witness. His voice was clear and vibrant as he gave his name and background, and unfolded in careful detail the same story he had previously related to Calvert. While he talked, his bold blue eyes were on the jurors, looking at them in the easy way of unsullied truth. His manner was calm and dignified, without a trace of the flippant or smart-alecky. His voice sank when he told of his dying mother and little brothers who waited in expectation of Christmas. The same voice was strong, confident, and unyielding in response to a fiery cross-examination by the outraged attorney for the United

States. On no single point did he yield ground. Instead he used the harsh interrogation to restate and reemphasize previous testimony, doing so at precisely the places where a bit of underscoring was helpful.

When his testimony ended and he stepped down, Calvert concluded that his client was the most masterful witness he had ever seen in a courtroom.

The judge then instructed the jury, laying a bit too much emphasis on the sanctity of the law, Calvert feared. He directed the attorneys to sum up and Calvert strode to a point in front of the jury box. His emotions were mixed, somewhat like those of a man who is about to be hanged and knows that he deserves it. That story, he gloomed, was weak as well water, but still, one never could tell with *absolute* certainty. More than one juror had gazed longingly at the prohibited fluid, and after all, it was only a few days to Christmas—and jurors might soften their hearts somewhat at this most pleasant of seasons. Besides, he was proud of his fighting Scotch-Irish ancestry and here he was, in a perfectly outlandish situation, working without any hope of remuneration, but in defense of a young man sprung from the same emerald sod. "If they convict," he said to himself, "they'll beat two good men at the same time."

With the courage of a bantam rooster assailing a dozen game cocks, he drew himself to his full height and laid it on the line for the poor, wronged orphan boy from the wicked city.

He surmised that this was no time for fireworks and opened in a low and solemn voice. He knew several of the jurors personally and reminded them of the fact. He spoke of the grave duty of a lawyer in a criminal case, a duty to present the case fully and fairly that justice might be done. He reminded them of their own immense responsibility to weigh all the evidence, to put aside prejudice, not to be influenced or overawed by the immense panoply and power of the federal government. He mentioned their duty to a stranger who enters their midst, as this young defendant had done, and quoted a few appropriate words from Jesus on the subject. There followed some comments about widows and the sons who aid them in their ill health and destitution. "A son who honors his mother," he said, his voice rising almost to a shout, "is not a liar and a rogue! The undisputed evidence in this case shows that the defendant is in the dock today because he remembered and obeyed God's holy commandment to love and support the dying woman who gave him birth!"

Calvert paused to let that shaft sink home and perceived that all the jurors were listening with rapt attention and that some of them were positively glaring their disapproval at the nettled district attorney.

Calvert resumed. There were more references to parents—to the dead father, the dying mother—and to the two little brothers whom someone would have to feed and clothe. "There are no hands for that task except those that were brought before you this morning, chained like the hands of a slave though no jury had yet declared him guilty of anything! Chained notwithstanding the presumption of innocence! Chained like a condemned man headed for the gallows before ever a judge or jury heard a single word from his own lips!"

He talked of holy constitutional safeguards and overzealous law officers who trample them underfoot. At this, more jurors began to glare at the prosecutor and the agents who sat with him at his mahogany counsel table. Then Calvert took up the subject of wicked men who tempt the young and innocent into crime, destroying them for their own vile profit. Juries, he reminded them, must stand as a shield to make certain such malignant ruses do not succeed. Only juries could prevent the unscrupulous from ensnaring unknowing young men in diabolical plots calculated to ruin them, while the real malefactors stayed safely hidden to count their corrupt lucre. Such men have always existed, he murmured. "One of them was named Judas, and he betrayed Jesus Christ."

He reminded them that they were bound by an oath to try the case according to the evidence alone. The evidence stood uncontradicted. It was true that the truck was loaded with whiskey and the defendant was driving it. Likewise there was no dispute about how the accused came to be there. "This mighty government with all its money and men has not brought you a word of testimony from anybody that this boy has lied to you! The district attorney wants you to *guess* that he lied, and then send him to the penitentiary for it."

Calvert directed a few words at the Harlan County merchant whom he suspected to be the strongest personality on the jury. Calvert knew that he had been orphaned in infancy, had grown up with his grandparents, and had lost his eldest son at Argonne Forest. He alluded to the sorrow and handicap of growing up without the counsel of a father to guide one in shunning evil influences. Young men just like this one had died by thousands on the gory fields of France to make the country safe for democracy. Democracy would be used to poor ends if that same kind of lad went to prison while the real wrongdoers walked the streets. In that event, those legions of fallen boys would have died in vain.

He ended with Christmas, then only a week away. "A special feeling is in the land at this time of year, a feeling that softens passions and makes people better," he said. "Our Saviour died to bring that spirit into the world for the benefit of all people everywhere. The quickest way to choke off the life of that widow in Chicago is to take away her boy. If Christmas morning finds her son in prison instead of by her side, he will never go back to her arms. When the prison doors open for him it will be too late to visit her bedside. He will visit her grave instead!"

On this histrionic note he sat down. The jury sat silent and unmoving. Obviously he had given them things to ponder and they were pondering them.

The district attorney shot to his feet as if rocket-propelled. He rushed to the lectern and opened with a voice that quavered with indignation. "Gentlemen of the jury, I have practiced law for a good many years, before numerous judges and hundreds of juries. I can say without a shadow of a doubt that the defendant's yarn in this case is the most fantastic cover-up for a crime I have ever heard, anywhere, anytime. And, in the same class with it, his counsel has begged you to turn him loose and let him go back to his wholesale bootlegging just because he says his mother is sick! My God, gentlemen, we don't *know* that he has a mother. She may have died years ago. She may have been the one who sent him on this outlandish journey in the first place. We do know, though, that he was arrested while driving along with nearly a hundred and fifty gallons of moonshine whiskey! The only connection this case has with the Christmas spirit was the stuff in those jars. It was intended for the Christmas trade in the Chicago speakeasies and, in my opinion, if the government agents hadn't caught him when they did, this defendant with his innocent-looking blue eyes would have been there behind the counter on Christmas Eve doling it out to the customers for two dollars a drink! "

There was considerably more in the same vein. Derision, ridicule, and venom was dumped on the defendant as the prosecutor retraced the trip from "that imaginary cold-water flat" to the poolroom, across two states to the "moonshine whiskey mills of Tennessee." He concluded with a wag of his finger under the defendant's nose, and, "He's innocent all right! Yes, indeed, he is. Just as innocent as Judas Iscariot was when he went out and hanged himself! "

The jury was out about forty minutes, and Calvert agonized in the torment of suspense known only to trial lawyers. His client was composed and calm. He spoke only once, to thank his attorney for trying so hard to save him. "Don't give up," Calvert admonished, "Uncle Sam has not won this case yet. "

When the jury returned, the merchant—he of the orphaned boyhood and fallen son—was in the lead clutching the written verdict. A hush fell as the verdict was handed up to the judge, who read it and passed it over to the clerk. "Is this your verdict, gentlemen?" Judge Cochran asked. All murmured, "It is, Your Honor. "

The clerk cleared his voice, adjusted his glasses, and read, "We, the jury, do agree and find the defendant not guilty on all counts of the indictment. "

It was the end of the day, and the dejected revenue agents

63

and the district attorney filed wearily from the room, frustration stamped in the sag of their shoulders. Calvert took his new friend, now free and visibly elated, aside for a final word. "You were lucky this time, son, but luck runs out. The next jury may put you in the jail and throw away the keys. Don't tempt fate, don't push your luck!"

The strong young hand came out to shake Calvert's in a firm, convincing grip. "Thanks for the advice as much as for all the rest you have done for me. This lesson was a hard one, but I will never forget it." The steadfast blue eyes gazed into Calvert's own. "An experience like this lasts a lifetime. All I want now is to get home and find a job. The straight and narrow is the road for me!" Then with a twinkle, "No more poolroom sessions of any kind."

Calvert pulled out his thin wallet and handed him a ten-dollar bill. "This will buy you some food along the way. I suppose you already know how to hobo and hitchhike."

"I'll make it," he replied, "and I will see that you get your money back. I'm down on my luck now, but someday I will have a job and wages. When that day comes you will be paid for what you did today. You will not lose a cent on this day's work."

Calvert left him in front of the courthouse. "Tell your mother and two little brothers that I send them a Christmas greeting in the words of Tiny Tim, 'God bless us every one!'" At the corner when he turned to look back through the gloom of the December dusk the youth still stood on the courthouse steps, the ten-dollar bill in his fingers, gazing after his benefactor. Each waved at the other in a final good-bye.

In the days that followed, Calvert's heart glowed with the warmth that comes only from good works. He had taken on a hard and thankless task, had prevailed against heavy odds, and had seen justice done. Doubtless his conduct had brought joy to a Chicago widow, but it had added nothing to his purse. When he returned to his own wife and tiny son, his prospects were as unpromising as before.

So the days passed. The weather was unusually gray and cold. His boy—little Cleon, Jr.—had been prepared for the likelihood that Saint Nick would bring few gifts this year. All had accepted their straitened circumstances with good grace. Anyway, with the spring the economy would improve, fees would flow again, the bleak times would lift. Despite all that had happened, Lord Calvert was a hopeful man.

Christmas came on Tuesday that year. On Sunday he got up early and went to church. The sermon dealt with the gift of the Magi, and the carols included *Silent Night, Good King Wenceslas, Away in a Manger,* and *I Heard the Bells on Christmas Day.* Calvert enjoyed the musical program and, as it ended, congratulated himself that even those who were pinched for money could share in this, the best part of the yuletide. When the congregation had dispersed he went to his office and picked up the *Courier-Journal* an ambitious paperboy had left by his door. On the way home he stopped at the post office and checked his mailbox. He twirled the dial on the old-fashioned combination lock, and the little door swung outward on its hinges. He peeped within. There was a single thin white envelope.

He opened the tiny letter knife at the end of his goldwatch chain and slit the end of the envelope. There was no return address but the envelope bore a Chicago postmark. He drew out the contents and blinked in amazement. Then he realized that there really is a good Spirit of Christmas that comforts those who do justice and truly believe. What he held in his fingers was a long, slender check, printed on expensive blue paper and drawn on a Chicago bank. It read: "Pay to the Order of Cleon K. Calvert the sum of $2,500."

It was signed, "Al Capone."

Attached to the check by a paper clip was a crisp new ten-dollar bill.

The War

IN THE HILLS many and marvelous are the tales that are told about "the war." Five times the nation has gone to war since Appomattox but in the mountains those are remembered as lesser conflicts when they are remembered at all. The Civil War, the War between the States, the War for Southern Independence, the War of the Rebellion—the old-timers called it by many names but always they remembered it with horror. In Appalachia generally, and in eastern Kentucky in particular, the struggle degenerated into a bloody and protracted contest between civilian factions. Long before Lee's surrender Yankee sympathizers were killing "rebels," and vice versa. Regiments of the two armies passed through the region on raids headed for Virginia or for the Kentucky Bluegrass and Ohio. They foraged for supplies, a practice the populace considered arrant robbery, and were mercilessly "bushwhacked" in retaliation. This led to the capture and execution of hostages which, in turn, generated more bushwhackers. By the end of the war the land and populace had been plundered back to primal poverty, internecine feuds were raging that would not die out entirely for fifty years, and political lines were drawn that have persisted to this day.

Modern highways and out-migration, radio, television, and consolidated schools have erased many of the old memories and traditions, but a quarter of a century ago the old recollections were still vivid. Though the guns had been stilled for nearly ninety years, the passions they had aroused still smoldered.

In 1953 I was the Democratic nominee for state representative in the Ninety-second District. The district embraced only

Letcher County. The upper reaches of Beef Hide Creek were almost roadless at that time and constituted a separate precinct. On an electioneering trip I stopped at a small, old-fashioned country store and heard a couple of unusual tales.

The building was a "boxed" affair with a tin roof and a porch that extended along the entire front. Steps led to the porch from the ruts and potholes that served as a road. Coca-Cola and Clabber Girl Baking Powder signs and a huge thermometer were nailed to the wall near the door. A tall potbellied stove stood in the center of the room inside, amid a circle of nail kegs and homemade chairs. Battered counters ran the length of the room and behind them were a soft-drink cooler and shelves of shoes, overalls, print dress materials, candy, chewing gum, canned goods, patent medicines, guns and cartridges, horse collars, assorted hardware, and school supplies. This emporium had provided an ample living for Willard and Minnie Burke through forty-five years and they were still there when I stopped by to ask them for their votes. An October chill was in the air and a coal fire crackled in the much-stained stove. Several men and an elderly woman sat around it enjoying the warmth and telling yarns about elections past. All received my cards and pleas that they vote for me, the Democrats nodding sympathetically and the Republicans withholding comment. The grandmotherly loafer looked at my card, pondered a moment, then asked me to take a chair at her side. She was about seventy-five and her wrinkled face was kind and gentle.

"I know your opponent," she said, "and I know a whole lot about you, though this is the first time we have met. I think it will be best for the county if you are elected and I sincerely hope you will win, but I just can't vote for you. My hands are tied and I will have to vote against you!"

I was puzzled by her comment and asked for an explanation. This is what she told me.

Her grandfather's name was Fayette Bentley and during the war he remained neutral and uncommitted. He had a farm on Beef Hide Creek—in fact the store building stood on a corner of

67

it—and he and his wife and children lived there in a "double-pen" cabin he had carved from tulip poplar trees. He and his family labored for their bread and the idea of human slavery was repugnant to them. Still, he did not join the Union army. There were five children under his roof and "Little Fayette," as he was called, was occupied fulltime in feeding and clothing them. He had no desire to orphan his children in one of the melancholy battles that were grinding Americans to dust by the tens of thousands. When the war was discussed, he said nothing. When recruiters "drummed for volunteers," he did not respond.

All went pretty well for him until the fall of 1864. In December, Ephraim Ratliff and a band of his men came home from the war in Virginia. Three years earlier Ben Caudill had recruited a regiment of young, hard, enthusiastic mountaineers to fight for the Confederacy. Since then most of his command had perished in battle or in hellish northern prisons. The youthful "Colonel Ben" had aged by decades and his shoulders had taken on a weary stoop. His proud young volunteers had turned thin and leathery. Their bodies were lean to emaciation, their clothing tattered, their horses little more than dispirited bone-bags. Only their weapons were still gleaming and well kept. The Thirteenth Kentucky Cavalry was preparing for its last fight.

Ratliff was a captain in that fateful year of the war. He and a few of his men had come home on Christmas furloughs, hoping to plow some cropland for spring planting before they returned. In the early spring when the final struggle would be joined they would go back to their commands. "Eph" Ratliff had become cruel and bitter in three years of warfare, but neither he nor the men who rode with him would surrender until the Confederacy was dead.

In January and February they scoured the Big Sandy Valley in search of "states-rights men" who would serve the South, but volunteers were few. The handwriting was on the wall; only the fanatical could still believe the rebellion might yet succeed. Most young men of Confederate leanings simply hid in the hills until the "recruiters" were gone. Too many older brothers had perished already, and with their passing the war lost its glamour. When Eph Ratliff headed for Lee's army in early March his band had gained only a handful of new members. The Confederacy was in its last throes.

Fayette Bentley was plowing a field with a bony horse, the only draft animal the foraging armies had left to him, on the brisk bright day when the rebels headed south again. They rode up meandering Beef Hide Creek to avoid the Unionist bush-whackers who lurked along the main road on Elkhorn Creek. When they saw the hapless Bentley they reined in and brusquely summoned the farmer. The Confederacy needs men, Ratliff told him, and he must go with them. He would be allowed to volunteer if he would; otherwise he would stand drafted as of this moment. Bentley's arguments were dismissed with oaths and imprecations, and the pleas and tears of his wife and children were overruled in the same fashion. Within ten minutes Bentley was riding the reluctant nag in a cause he abhorred, toward a battlefield he feared and for which he was totally unprepared by any training.

They crossed the Pine Mountain and camped near the Pound River in Wise County, Virginia. It was a rendezvous for mountain rebels assembling for their last campaign, and all afternoon and far into the night little bands of gaunt, ragged men straggled in. Near midnight a dozen old campaigners arrived, and Fayette Bentley took advantage of the excitement of the moment to slip away into the darkness. Through the rest of the night he toiled afoot up the laurel-choked south side of the Pine, then down the boulder-strewn Kentucky side. He followed the ridge tops to the head of Beef Hide Creek and pursued the stream to his cabin door. A little after sunup his wife and children were delighted to see him stumble out of the woods, thoroughly happy notwithstanding the cuts and bruises acquired in his nocturnal journey. But their jubilation was short-lived. He had scarcely had time to hug the last of his children when Ratliff's horsemen encircled the house and commanded him to come out. What followed was sheer horror.

Ratliff was in a towering rage. "Goddamn you, Bentley, we gave you a chance to be a man and fight for the greatest cause in history, and you ran away like a coward. Now you've got to die like a coward. There is no room in this world for a Goddamned deserter!"

Bentley, his wife, and his cowering children all knew at once that entreaty was useless. The fugitive drew himself up with manly courage and asked that he be allowed a few minutes to pray. Ratliff acceded to this request and the condemned man knelt on his own doorstep, Ratliff standing behind him with a cocked revolver in his hand. Bentley's lips moved in silent entreaty. There was no sound except the sobbing of his daughters. Suddenly his executioner said, "Damn you, you have prayed long enough!" and the long-barreled Colt boomed.

Ratliff swung into his saddle and the rebels clattered away. His victim writhed and twisted, a huge hole in the back of his head. His oldest child, a thirteen-year-old daughter, held his head until his limbs convulsed in a final spasm. His pale-faced and tight-lipped wife watched him die, knowing that she was unable to help him in any way.

The widow and children dug a grave. They washed the body clean of blood and wrapped it in a shroud made of new linsey-woolsey. They had no coffin and no way to make one, so Fayette Bentley went to his long sleep in no other covering. His benumbed widow planted corn in the field he had plowed on the last day of his life.

A month passed and word came that the "Slave-Power" was broken. Lee had surrendered and the war was over. Then one day when the corn shoots were a few inches out of the ground the "Widow Bentley" heard the creak of saddle leather and the clink of horseshoes on the stony road. The band that rode past had been reduced by half and the survivors were hollow-eyed scarecrows. Ephraim Ratliff was in the lead, his bony shoulders poking up through his ragged coat, his eyes glazed with fatigue and hopelessness. Like thousands of men all over the South, these rebels had come home.

Ratliff's house was twenty miles away in broad, rich bottom-lands not at all like the pinched farm on Beef Hide Creek. The widow could visualize his homecoming to a farm swept free of slaves. The war and its miseries had accomplished that much at least. If Eph Ratliff's place were to be farmed he would have to do it with his own hands and his own sweat. But the widow did not want him to farm those fertile bottoms at all. She had other hopes for him.

That night she gathered her five children around her bed and asked them to kneel with her. In a low, compelling voice she asked Almighty God to look down upon her, and to hear and grant her prayer. "Kill Eph Ratliff, O Lord. Do not let him live here in the sight of my fatherless children and be a reproach to them. He is wicked past understanding, and I pray that you will strike him dead! "

Two days later a man named Hogg came up the road. He lived far away in another part of the county and had been a Confederate soldier. He had been to Louisa to surrender to federal authorities, to renounce all treason and take an oath of true allegiance to the United States. He told her about happenings down the Big Sandy. Then he mentioned Captain Ratliff.

The widow looked up questioningly. "What about Captain Ratliff? " she inquired.

"He is dead, " was the answer. "He got home from the war night afore last. He had his supper and went to bed. When he woke up yesterday morning he sat on the side of the bed for a minute or two. All of a sudden he grabbed at his chest and let out a little squawking sound, then fell over dead. He never said a single word. "

The widow Bentley smiled, then went inside the house and knelt. She thanked God for his generosity. She had never doubted that he would answer her prayer.

"You see, " the good woman told me eighty-eight years after the cavalry captain came to the end of his trail, "I am the daughter of Fayette Bentley's oldest daughter, the one who was thirteen when he was killed. My grandmother lived thirty-five years after that, and a a girl growing up I spent many nights with her. She told me all about the war and how my grandfather was killed.

"She asked me to promise that I would not forget the war or the rebels who caused it. She said they were all Democrats and never to be trusted. She said that someday women would be given the right to vote, and when I was twelve years old I promised her I would never—under any circumstance—vote for a Democrat! "

She smiled at me and her face softened.

"So, now you understand why I can't vote for you, but I will ask God to see that you are elected. He answered my grandmother's prayer and I believe he will grant mine, too. "

She patted my arm in a most confident and knowing way.

After thanking her for her promised prayers I took my leave. Another of the loafers—a man of seventy-five or more, in patched overalls, and with the aroma of moonshine whiskey about him—followed me from the store. His name was Wright, and he assured me that while "the old lady's" vote was lost to me, I could certainly count on receiving his own. He asked me to follow him up the road a few hundred yards to the mouth of a small tributary stream flowing in from a narrow hollow. There the creek bottoms were not wide but the fescue and clover were as green as emerald.

He pointed out the old-fashioned weatherboarded house where he lived, and said that a portion of it was a log structure enclosed by the planking. His grandfather had built it before the war and lived on the farm when he joined the rebel army. He fought in "Rebel John" Morgan's command and was captured in 1864 at Gladeville, Virginia. A few months later he swore to take up arms no more against the United States and was paroled. He scrupulously obeyed the terms of his release and came back to his home and family.

He had been here at work in his fields when Union soldiers came by, looking for members of Eph Ratliff's company. They cocked their rifles and demanded that he come to them, their commanding officer saying that he never knew a "turn-coat rebel son-of-a-bitch who obeyed his parole." Another declared, "Once a rebel always a rebel!" and flourished his saber. His grandfather had never served with Ratliff or even in the same battalion, but it was apparent this would do him no good. He ducked behind his plow mule and fled for the timber at the top of the hill.

"My grandpap was a fast runner, and granny said he could dodge like a fox, so their whole volley missed him. The balls kicked up dirt all around him and it looked to his family fer a minute or two that he would make it to the big rocks and ivy thickets on the other side of the ridge. There he could lay up fer weeks and never be found."

But his luck did not hold. Wright showed me where a tall red cedar gatepost had once stood—it had lasted, in fact, until after 1910. One of the soldiers had a new kind of rifle and he laid it against the post to steady his aim as he drew a fine bead along the octagonal barrel. "He stood right where you air now and shot my granddaddy in the back with a Sharp's needle gun!"

"So, don't feel too bad about losin' the old woman's vote. I never go to vote without passin' where the gatepost stood, and I never pass it without thinkin' what happened there. And that is why I have voted for fifty-five years without ever once markin' a ballot for a Republican!"

"But," he murmured with a melancholy sigh, "I can't do a thing in the world with my wife. We just cancel out one another's vote every time an election comes around. You can see from what she told you that she is as stubborn as hell!"

Another story concerning the Civil War brought me to the only ghost I have ever encountered. And while I still do not believe in ghosts I must admit that I heard one's footsteps and the sound made my skin crawl in a most memorable manner.

Byrd Ison kept a country store near the mouth of Defeated Creek. He was a real gentlemen, and travelers along that isolated creek were fortunate indeed to find themselves by his fireside on blustery nights. Mrs. Ison was an excellent cook and hostess, and her meals were legendary. In my boyhood my father and I used to find business in that section of the county so we could spend the night with the Isons and sleep in the immense featherbeds in the huge upstairs rooms. Each room had a fireplace with a coal grate, and the combination of soft featherbed, flickering firelight, and rain drumming on the tin roof induced sleep of a kind no modern hostelry can hope to provide.

On one such visit in early spring Mr. Ison told me about the family ghost. He said it had haunted the house since "war times." No one had seen it but many people had heard it. "You'll sleep upstairs tonight and in the morning if you wake up just as daylight comes you will hear it, too. The ghost walks back and forth, back and forth, from one end of the porch to the other, every morning just at the edge of day. I have heard it thousands of times."

He said that the house was built in slavery times, an old-fashioned, L-shaped, two-story frame structure. His uncle had served in the Union army, joining as a mere stripling. "Somewhere in old Virginye" he had become desperately sick and had lingered near death for many days. When he was able to travel he was furloughed and came home for a month. A friend of about the same age—a young man from Ohio—had accompanied him. They made a splendid sight on their black cavalry horses, in new blue uniforms, each armed with a Colt revolver, a saber, and a .60 caliber carbine. The joy with which Ison's parents welcomed them was tempered by the knowledge that bushwhackers swarmed the countryside, endangering the lives of all soldiers in both uniforms.

The soldiers occupied those two huge, high-ceilinged rooms with doors that opened on the upstairs porch. Their furlough passed pleasantly, and the day came when they must ride back across the intervening hills to the army at Cumberland Gap. Both rose early, washed, shaved, and ate breakfast. Young Ison went to the barn to bring down the horses his father had already fed, saddled, and bridled. Dawn was creeping across the timbered hills, its pale misty light touching the treetops, then the cliffy ridges, then stealing softly into the coves and hollows. The young soldier from Ohio waited on the porch, striding with measured steps from banister to banister. His cavalry boots caused the floorboards to crack against their nails as he walked, pausing occasionally to listen for the horses. The light crept to the chimney tops, then touched the porch. There was a pause as the soldier turned, then—crack! A rifle sounded from a nearby ridge and the soldier collapsed, a huge, hollow lead bullet in his heart. A pro-rebel bushwhacker had made certain that a northern mother would wait in vain for her son.

He was buried in the Ison family cemetery. A marker was set up over his grave but no name was carved on it. Young Ison went back to the war and returned when it ended. He married, raised a family, grew old, and died. The name of his fallen friend was forgotten. The identity of the bushwhacker was never discovered.

Byrd Ison inherited the farm and he too grew old. His children came, reached adulthood and went away. Through it all the murdered soldier kept his dawn vigil. "He will be there when I am dead and gone," Mr. Ison concluded as we prepared for bed.

I slept in that incomparable bed in the same room that had sheltered one of the youthful soldiers so long ago. The old-fashioned door still opened on the same porch. I slept through a dream-filled night in which soldiers in blue uniforms rode spirited horses to pleasant farmhouses. The next morning I suddenly awakened fully alert and with a realization that dawn was at hand.

Chickens were crowing on their distant roosts. Birds twittered in the huge cedars in the front yards. The ripple of water came up from the rocky bottom of the creek. I listened intently as the light increased so that the dim outline of trees could be made out. With every vestige of logic I could muster I assured myself that no footsteps would be heard. I knew—and now know—there are no ghosts that outlive the flesh to return to former haunts. But still—and suddenly there was that sound! A board creaked outside the door, and then another. With the cadence of a healthy man striding over them, the old planks groaned against their ancient nails. Back and forth, up and down, pause. The eerie sound repeated itself a dozen times. I sat up in bed, pulled aside the soft lace curtain and looked out. Nothing moved. The hickory-bottomed chairs were undisturbed. The sound came again, the timing unaltered. Then the sunlight touched the highest crag on the Pine Mountain, sparrows and cardinals flew from their trees, and the boards were stilled.

I lay for a time pondering the phenomenon. Perhaps changing atmospheric conditions caused the planks to expand. Maybe they had absorbed moisture during the night and this had brought about displacement. The old foundation stones might be settling, so that the porch sagged. There were many possibilities.

At breakfast my host smiled. "You heard him, didn't you? He never wakes anyone up, but if a body is already awake he will hear his footsteps, He never fails to come."

The old house still stands. Byrd Ison has joined his father in the neglected cemetery, and the rumble of coal trucks has shattered the rural stillness he enjoyed for so many years. Perhaps the old boards still creak in the first light of dawn. It is more likely, I think, that they are silent. Ghosts will not walk where there is no one to hear.

When I met Sie Cornett I was thirteen and he was a hale and hearty eighty-five. My father, our friend Wilson Fields, and I stopped at Sie's ancient cabin to ask him to play his fife for us. He had joined the Union army at fourteen and been trained as a fifer. He had "played for the soldiers many and many a day" and had accompanied the Army of the Potomac to numerous memorable encounters, including second Manassas, Gettysburg, and Cold Harbor. He said he had seen "a sight of bloodshed."

When he came home he never married but stayed on with "Ma and Pa" until they died. He had lived alone at the old hewed-log cabin for forty years. He drew a "war pension," farmed a little, dug ginseng "when the market was right," and, when the mood was on him, played his fife. Sometimes travelers on the county road would hear him calling ghostly formations to Assembly or Retreat.

Sie brought out the wooden cylinder that had been handed to him in 1861 and showed it to me. He pointed to the letters "U. S." imprinted in the hard dark wood and inserted the brass mouthpiece. He poured a dipper of water into the tube, then shook it out. His dark eyes glittered in his cadaverous face. He smiled, showing a few remaining teeth, yellowed with the smoke of countless pipes. "I will play you the tune the soldiers liked best to hear," he said.

He lifted the fife, blew through it, and piped the thin, shrill notes of "Jenny Get Around." For my information he then sang the words in a high cracked voice:

Jenny get around, Jenny get around,
Jenny get around, I say!
Jenny get around, Jenny get around
On a long summer's day!

"I played that at Gettysburg," he mused, "but the rebels was a-yellin' so loud, and the Yankees was a-cussin' and a-swearin' and a-shootin', so that I couldn't even hear it myself."

He played brisk marches and a slow funeral dirge. Then out of his fife came a lovely sound which he called "Piping the Birds Down out of the Trees." When his old lungs were tired he told me about Cold Harbor.

"The rebels was in trenches the devil must have dug fer them. Deep and with dugouts a shell couldn't shake. The guns blasted them so long that a man couldn't see where they lay. Then the order came for the musicians to 'fife them out.'

"That was the grandest army I ever seen when they went against the rebs at Cold Harbor. Squads, platoons, companies, regiments, divisions, all in good order and movin' fast. They rushed the Southern lines to break through before the smoke and dust could clear. Even the officers carried rifles with bayonets set. They went in a wild rush, every man screamin' fer blood. If they had broke through, the war would have ended that day.

"But the Democrats stood firm in them devilish trenches. Every man had four or five rifles, and the wounded loaded fer the well. The muskets popped in a steady roar and kept it up like a hot wind. The government soldiers fell by the thousands, and when the army come runnin' back the ground was covered with blue. I can see it yit!"

He filled his corncob pipe. "They piled back into our lines, wore out and droopin' tired. Our artillery went off agin and the rebels caught it fer a solid hour. Then the messengers come and said that when the fire slacked off we must fife them out agin. I stood on the parapet and marched in place with my back to the Democrats, and fifed and fifed and fifed. I played every tune I could remember: all I had learned from the musicians and all I knowed from back home, but nothing happened. The captains and lieutenants and sergeants tried, but they couldn't get the men to charge a second time. They just plain wouldn't go. After a while the fifers got out of breath, too, and got down behind the parapets, and the battle of Cold Harbor was over.

"General Grant asked fer a truce and we carried in the dead and wounded. The rebels helped us pick up some that had got to the edge of their rifle pits. Them rebels was skin and bones, and nearly barefooted. I never seed a scarecrow with such sorry clothes on."

He put the old fife back inside its old case. "But, O Lord, how they could shoot!"

Twenty years later when Sie had long since fifed his last tune I told his story to Larcena Hogg, who as a dimpled damsel of sixteen had married Steve Hogg, one of Lee's cavalrymen. By the time Cold Harbor was fought, his horse was dead and he had joined the infantry. A man of means when the war began, he was slaveless and destitute at its end. "Steve didn't have any shoes when he got home and had to go to the woods and kill a groundhog for its hide. He used it to make some moccasins and wore them when he walked to Louisa to surrender. He took the oath of allegiance and started back home. His moccasins wore out on the way and he come the last twenty miles barefooted."

Her tired old eyes were reflective as she remembered the words the thirty-year-old veteran had told his girlish bride. "Steve said the war was hell on earth. He went hungry most of the time for four years, and slept on the ground like a dog. He was cold in the wintertime, and scorched in the summertime, and sometimes he was mighty sick. His friends was killed until only a few was left. He lost all of his slaves and come back home a barefooted pauper. But Steve said, 'By God, Cold Harbor made it all worth while. The way we shot down the blue necks that day paid for every bit of it!'"

John Lucas was eighty-nine when he died in 1969. "Uncle John," as he was called, was beloved throughout the county. He was diminutive, with kindly eyes and a curling, bristly beard. But there was iron in this man, because he helped to organize the United Mine Workers in Harlan and Bell counties and that took much courage. One of his co-workers in that era paid him a mighty compliment: "John Lucas could look the devil in the face and not flinch."

Uncle John told me stories about Martin Van Buren Bates, whom he called "the giant," and explained why he could never stay in the hills after the war. John was distantly related to him and had seen him several times.

Martin Van Buren Bates was born in 1845 and grew prodigiously. When he was full grown he was seven feet eleven inches tall and weighed 478 pounds. He was fully developed intellectually and physically and except for his immense size and strength, was in no sense freakish. After the war he joined a circus and traveled widely in performances that featured the famous dwarf Tom Thumb. A gigantic carriage was built for Bates and he rode triumphant in it through many cities. In London Queen Victoria was so taken by his winsome ways that she presented him with a pocket watch as large as a small alarm clock.

His Nova Scotia–born wife was an inch taller than he. According to Robert Ripley's syndicated column *Believe It or Not* their twenty-two-pound boy was the largest baby born alive to any couple of whom a record has survived.

He was a cousin of Bad John Wright, the crack marksman, who traveled with him in "The Greatest Show on Earth." He served in the Confederate army with John and was captured at Gladeville, Virginia, when his agile and quick-witted kinsman escaped.

Uncle John said that the giant was taken to Washington and put on display by the Union army. The soldiers marched him through the street for the edification of the populace. President Lincoln was told about "the big rebel" and took Mrs. Lincoln on a carriage ride to see the unusual prisoner. Bates greeted the president pleasantly and they had a delightful conversation. "How is the weather up there above my head?" asked the president, who was no runt himself. "Fine," answered the giant. "How is it down there below my navel?"

Martin Van Buren Bates was not always the courteous and kindly giant who so pleased good Queen Victoria and bantered with the president. During the war he used two colossal .71-caliber horse pistols that had been made especially for him at the Tredegar Iron Works at Richmond. He wore them strapped across his chest in black leather holsters. He had a saber that was eighteen inches longer than the standard weapon. He rode a huge Percheron horse that he took from a German farmer in Pennsylvania. His courage and daring matched his size and cunning.

When he was paroled on a sworn pledge to fight no more against the United States, he returned to the hills and found them in turmoil. A band of local Unionists had captured one of the giant's brothers—a brother of the redoubtable "Black Rob" Bates also—and had tied him to a tree and bayoneted him to death. The man's widow told Martin Van Buren how her husband had died painfully and slowly beneath the slender blades. The giant's eyes hardened.

Despite his youth the giant had been elected a captain, and he continued to serve as such after his parole, which was soon violated. He put on the uniform his mother and two other women made for him out of homespun wool, buckled on the gigantic sword and pistols, and mounted the Pennsylvanian's commandeered horse. He gathered his men and they went to wreak vengeance upon the murderers of their comrade and kinsman.

One by one their quarry were captured. Some were roused out of their beds at night. Others were found hiding in hilltop caverns. Some were ambushed on the trails. All were taken to a log corncrib on Rock House Creek and locked in it under close and continuous guard. Then their wives, parents, grandparents, and children were rounded up and driven to the mouth of Big Hollow and kept there around campfires all night. The children ranged from about twelve years old down to babies in their mothers' arms. Some of the wives were pregnant.

Two slender blackoaks grew a dozen feet apart. A pole was lashed to the trees about ten feet up. A round beech log was cut, stripped of its branches, and placed on the ground beneath. Eight nooses hung down from the pole.

At dawn the rebels roused the sleepers, who threw fresh wood on the fires. At the sight of the dangling ropes the women began to wail. The giant appeared on his giant horse, his giant sword and pistols gleaming, his black eyes shining with contempt and hatred. His men appeared out of the gloomy mists herding the prisoners before them, each man's hands bound behind his back.

The prisoners were placed on the log, and a noose was dropped around each shrinking neck. The men pleaded for their lives. Their relatives begged the giant to be merciful. The giant sat on his great horse for several minutes while dawn slowly brightened the sky. The fire crackled, adding its gleams to the soft light of the new day. The killers began to hope a little; then the giant raised his hand in a signal. Two men gave the log a shove and it rolled down the hill. The eight bound figures dropped a few inches and choked slowly to death. With swords and cocked pistols the women and children were kept at bay. None could render aid.

The "Yankees" were a quarter of an hour dying. When the last body had ceased to jerk and twitch, the giant spoke. He told the people not to touch the dead or take them down from the gallows. They were to hang there and rot by the road, their corruption warning all passersby of the consequences of killing a Bates. If anyone violated his order he would go to the same gibbet and die in the same way. Absolutely no mercy would be shown. In addition, his family would be destroyed, his house burned, his stock killed. "Take warning," the giant said, "because no other warning will be given!" Then he and his men rode away, leaving the dead to swing in the wind and their kin to mourn them through a monstrous nightmare.

The bodies turned to skeletons before the giant came back from the final battles. Only rattling bones were left for burial.

Uncle John said the giant could not stay in Letcher County after that. "When those children got old enough they would have killed him without a doubt. He moved away when the war was over and didn't tell people where he went, either. You know what *his* vengeance was like. We can't even guess what those children would have done to even the score when they got to be grown men."

The Marriage of
Samuel Tate

SAM TATE, as I shall call him, was my client for several years before a well-aimed bullet ended his career in 1963. Into his sixty-three years he jammed an astounding number of felonies, misdemeanors, and escapades. He shot three men to death (one of them his brother), and on three separate occasions heard himself sentenced to the state penitentiary for the rest of his natural life. Obviously these solemn judicial pronouncements were of scant effect, for he was repeatedly pardoned or paroled and, as our rehabilitation experts say, was returned to society. He explained to me just how the system works. "The more money you have the more justice you get. If you plan to kill somebody, be sure to get plenty of money together first."

Sam had plenty of money. After the repeal of Prohibition he opened a roadhouse on Tunnel Hill east of Whitesburg. It was called the Bloody Bucket Inn and on one occasion when I was a college student he admitted me to its unholy confines. In a back room there was an enormous brass bed. Sam introduced me to his wife Maxie, and to his "concubine," Elizabeth. He explained his sleeping arrangements. He found repose in the middle, with his wife on his right side and his concubine on his left.

Soon after this memorable conversation, big, blond, bosomy Elizabeth shot small, slender Maxie to death "in self-defense." The grief-stricken widower collected Maxie's life insurance and used the money to hire defense counsel for Elizabeth. A jury fixed her punishment at five years imprisonment but the parole board set her free in much less time than that. The "reformed and penitent" Elizabeth returned to Whitesburg where she and Sam were promptly married. She wore the most and the largest diamonds I have ever seen displayed on any one person.

When his concubine became his wife, Sam was reveling in prosperity. World War II had ended, and an immense coal boom was under way. Sam had used his capital acquired at the Bloody Bucket to gain control of a coal dock. Hundreds of "truck mines" were operating, and Sam bought all the coal they could haul to him. He paid as little as he could induce his suppliers to accept, and then shipped it for resale at the highest price he could extract in the fuel-short market. When the war ended, Congress had abolished price controls, and coal prices were skyrocketing. Sam began wallowing in money, his operation shipping fifty or more cars daily.

Huge diamonds glittered on his fingers and a diamond-studded watch sparkled on his wrist. Elizabeth was draped in furs and drove a Packard. Sam loved thousand-dollar bills and sometimes had several hundred of them in the enormous leather wallet he carried in his hip pocket—a wallet that was bound to his waist belt by a length of steel chain. Other sums were stashed away in "secret places," and profits swelled when he succeeded in outlawing the sale of whiskey under the "local option" statutes and contrived to set himself up as "head bootlegger" to whom all lesser vendors were required to pay tribute. This arrangement aroused the indignation of his competitors, one of whom sneaked up under the cover of darkness and blasted his brand-new Packard sedan into tiny bits of scrap iron. His twenty-two licensed taxicabs carried the comforts of bootleg whiskey throughout the county, to the edification of all who possessed the purchase price.

Sam was a free spirit who loathed the idea of paying taxes, so he simply ignored the revenue laws. He kept all the profits of his coal and bootlegging operations in cash, filed no returns, and paid nothing. Finally the collectors caught up with him and made

84

a "net worth assessment of taxes due" amounting to several hundred thousand dollars. His lawyer bargained with IRS, and the agents agreed to settle for $75,000. Sam said that was still too much and offered $25,000. He explained that the coal boom would soon be over—all booms end in bust and that one crashed in 1948—and then money would not be easy to come by. The punishment would not exceed three years imprisonment and the government's proposal figured out to $25,000 per year—much more than he could take in during a coal depression. If IRS did not accept his offer, it would get nothing whatever. On this note he left the conference.

He was indicted, tried, and convicted, serving three years in a federal prison. While he was undergoing correction the government foreclosed its tax lien against all his property, and United States District Judge Mac Swinford ordered everything sold to satisfy the owner's tax delinquencies. A title search revealed that all they could find—houses, real estate, cars, coal properties—were under mortgage to Elizabeth Tate to secure immense loans. Sam's wife was summoned as a defendant in the foreclosure but filed no answer. Swinford adjudged the mortgage to Elizabeth Tate was fraudulent and void.

The sale was duly publicized as required by law. On the appointed day a large crowd of prospective purchasers gathered to hear the United States marshal offer the property at auction. As the marshal cleared his throat to begin, an old lady came forward clinging to the arm of her attorney. The lawyer made an announcement. His client was Elizabeth Tate, mother of the defendant, Sam Tate. She held the recorded mortgage against the property and had never been summoned in the foreclosure suit. She had learned of the projected sale that morning and had come to warn that her mortgage was valid. The wrong Elizabeth Tate had been summoned, the lawyer declared.

Under these circumstances not a single bid was received. IRS demanded to know where the eighty-six-year-old widow of Robert Tate had gotten so much money. From her husband, she said, who kept it in cash in a money belt around his waist, and handed it to her on his deathbed thirty years earlier. She had kept the money until "Samuel needed it to get into the coal business," and had lent it to him duly secured by the mortgage.

The government could never disprove this story. She sued, foreclosed her mortgage, and the properties were sold. The sale money came to her and she gave it in cash to Sam upon his release. He placed it with the tremendous sums he had previously stored away from the sale of coal and whiskey.

The government collected nothing. Sam saved $75,000. In the penitentiary he was treated well, he said. He was appointed straw boss of a gang of trusties. He did not have to work much himself but simply made sure the others kept busy.

Sam's criminal record filled several typewritten pages: three murder convictions, plus numerous indictments charging him with armed robbery, carrying concealed deadly weapons, shooting with intent to kill, income tax evasion, possessing an untaxed machine gun in violation of the federal revenue laws, assault and battery, making moonshine whiskey, selling untaxed alcoholic beverages, operating a roadhouse without a license, contributing to the delinquency of minors, adultery, seduction, operating a house of ill fame, permitting gambling on his premises, using the mails to defraud, statutory rape. In his last appearance as a defendant he was charged with the merest of misdemeanors—selling firecrackers.

On nearly all of these charges Sam was acquitted. Eyewitnesses swore he didn't do it or a juror obstinately insisted on acquittal. Sam loved what he called "pet jurors." After a "hung jury" or an acquittal such a "loyal, hard-working juror" generally appeared in a new Plymouth or Chevrolet. "Good works deserve good works," Sam said.

Still he spent much of his life behind bars, and his machinations often were thwarted. For example, a few years before his death I defended him against a felony charge. At the close of the trial Sam was unconcerned. He had, he said, "a special friend" on the jury. "I told him to hang the jury or die, and he gave me his word of honor that he would do it." The twelve men and women were out a long time debating the verdict. At last they filed back into the courtroom and reported themselves hopelessly deadlocked, divided eleven to one.

The jury was discharged and the case was rescheduled for a new trial at the next term. An hour or so later Sam popped into my office, his face livid with wrath. Referring to his "special friend," he reported that he had hung the jury. "All the others wanted to acquit," Sam fumed. "Just because I told him to hang it or die, that idiot wouldn't agree to anything but a hung jury. He wouldn't even agree to turn me loose scot-free!"

Then his face brightened with a new thought. "When this gets out to the public it will look bad on the prosecution. People will think somebody bribed him to convict me regardless of the evidence."

Some years later Sam undertook to extort some money from a "little two-by-four bootlegger from Harlan County." The man paid up three or four times, $100 at a clip. When Sam came to collect again, the enraged bootlegger shot him in the face with a .38 special revolver. Thus a man with many hundreds of thousands—perhaps millions—of dollars hidden away in cash died for a trifling sum.

His funeral was attended by a "host of mourners," according to the preacher. If his hidden money was found, it was found in silence and spent the same way. The sturdy Elizabeth had long since been divorced and a new wife instated in her place, but the grieving young widow professed ignorance of the hiding place. There were no children, and Sam's brothers and sisters expressed only mystification. Treasury agents lurked about for a while, but went away empty-handed. Somewhere a bag or box or drawer full of money moulders unspent.

Or was it left with a trusted friend who kept it with the same tightness of lip that Sam displayed, dipping into it cautiously and only as need arose? The whereabouts and extent of this cash fortune may never be known. Perhaps a carelessly started fire in some nondescript building has reduced it to ashes.

On the day of Sam's funeral a huge black Cadillac hearse carried his body to the cemetery, followed by a couple of dozen automobiles filled with mourners. As the cortege passed through Whitesburg, I was in conference with an aging woman who had grown up on Indian Fork of Rock House Creek. She watched the slow and dignified passage of the vehicles in silent distaste, her lips curled in unconcealed scorn. I asked her whether she had known the deceased and she allowed that she had. She could recall him as a little boy and as a lusty youth. "He was just as bad when he was a child as he was when he died. He never changed any at all in his real nature. There never was any limit to his devilment. "

She was reluctant to discuss him in detail, but under my questioning she opened up and told me about Sam's first "marriage," entered into more than forty years before he came to his violent end. It happened before either highway or railroad came to the Rock House section, when not one adult in ten could write his name, and most of the women had never been ten miles from their homes. Scratch farming and moonshining supported a frontier-style society in which a reincarnated Daniel Boone might have felt at home. Sam's bride was my visitor's cousin or sister, pure and innocent at eighteen. The groom was a husky nineteen and had not yet killed anyone, but displayed no symptom of either of the two qualities so characteristic of the girl.

We shall refer to the young woman as Nellie, and Sam became enamored of her when they met by chance at a country store. He was enticed by her splendid person, including flawless skin, white teeth, dimpled chin, and shapely neck. To these charms were added the allure of firm round breasts, exquisite legs, and rippling hips. Sam was enthralled.

In the manner of innumerable swains before and since, Sam attempted seduction but was rebuffed. The girl was warm-blooded but chaste. Hugs and kisses, yes, but absolutely no more. Sam was beside himself with frustration. Nellie found Sam interesting; after all, he was strong as a bear, healthy, good-looking, and persuasive. In addition—and of no small importance—his father was rich by the standards of the time and place. She made it clear that only matrimony was acceptable. She would be his only after a lawful marriage. She became explicit. "I mean married by a preacher on a license out of the courthouse. I won't have this business of layin' a broomstick down on the floor and steppin' across it together, then sayin' we're married. That just ain't for me."

Sam was baffled. He had not contemplated so drastic a step as marriage. He was not baffled for long, however. Within a few moments he bid her an affectionate farewell. He was, he explained, headed for Whitesburg for a marriage license. He would bring a preacher back with him and they would be married "this very day." By taking a shortcut down Thornton Creek he could make it to the county seat and back to her home by eight o'clock that night. They would be married at her father's three-room house, have a wedding supper, and then to bed.

The ecstatic young lady dashed away to tell her parents and other relatives about it all and to set things in order, while Sam mounted the chestnut saddle horse his father had given him and spurred away to the west. It was a cold day and the wind nipped at his flesh. Presently he dismounted to warm himself before the fire at the home of his brother Uriah.

Uriah was considerably older than Sam and had a brood of little ones well under way. As Sam sat by the blazing grate, he pondered the room and its comforting reminders of domestic stability and bliss. There was no question about it, "U.L." was on his way toward becoming an established and prosperous citizen.

On one wall was a lithographed picture of Jesus praying at Gethsemane, a shaft of light falling about him. On another wall was a photograph of Mrs. Tate's parents. Immediately above Mrs. Tate's treadle sewing machine was a framed etching of a bull. Sam used his sixth-grade education to decipher the ornately printed lines. They certified the pedigree of the pure-bred Jersey Uriah had bought a few months before in an effort to improve the quality of his own scrawny milk cows and those of his neighbors. Nearby on a dresser were a couple of blank forms which could be used to attest the blood line of the animal to anyone whose cow had been "serviced" by him. Uriah said he was a real calf-getter.

Sam cogitated on these things. Presently Uriah and his wife left the room for a few moments and Sam, properly warmed, followed them a little later. He remounted his horse and rode back up Rock House Creek. But now his heart was light and he hummed and whistled for joy. At the mouth of Sexton's Branch there lived an ordained preacher of the Old Regular Baptist persuasion. Sam knocked at his door and informed him of his intention to marry. The preacher was urged to saddle his mule and come along to perform the solemn rites. Sam slipped him a ten-dollar bill and promised him an honored place at the wedding table. Within minutes the mule was plodding along by Sam's horse while the minister congratulated Sam on his good fortune in finding so excellent a wife.

Sam knew that the preacher was illiterate. He didn't know a letter in any book and could scarcely scrawl his name, but this was no serious shortcoming. In Sam's view one preacher was as good as another when there was a marriage to be performed.

Besides, his delectable bride-to-be had never been to school a day in her life and was as untaught as her parents. On Rock House Creek in 1920, Sam's "learnin'" represented a major accomplishment of which he could be justly proud. It was one reason Nellie deemed him a splendid catch.

When they arrived at the bride's home she was astounded at his hasty return. Her face fell because he had not been gone long enough to have reached the county seat. But Sam did not falter. Cheerfully he waved the precious license and explained how by a happy chance he had met the county court clerk on the road and that genial official had issued the license on the spot. Nellie took the document and studied it intently, puzzlement in her eyes.

90

"Why," she murmured, "I thought in Kentucky a marriage license had a picture of two men shaking hands."

Sam had heard about the Seal of Kentucky. In its center was a picture of an urban man of business and a pioneer, hands joined in a friendly clasp; the two figures were bordered by the motto "United We Stand, Divided We Fall." But he had an explanation. "The legislature changed all of that," he explained. "This is the new way they make a marriage license."

He kissed the reassured girl and hugged her supple waist. Her heart overflowed with love and she returned his embrace.

The ladies had wrought havoc among the chickens and were cooking the dismembered carcasses on the wood-burning stove. Within an hour the family was seated for the feast, Sam and Nellie side by side and the preacher diligently at work across the table. All relished the chicken and dumplings, mashed potatoes, "shucky" beans, pickled corn, and hot biscuits. This was followed by a stack-cake made with gingerbread and dried apples. It was a happy group that gathered before the fire a few moments later to see the couple become one.

The preacher had the ceremony memorized and got through it tolerably well. When he had finished and Sam had bestowed a kiss of inordinate length on the bride, the groom took a pen and filled out the blank spaces in the license. He inserted names and dates and showed the preacher where to sign. The good man sat down, took the pen in hand, clamped his tongue between his teeth in deep concentration and, after a false start or two, produced an erratic squiggle that represented his signature. Soon afterwards he rode away on the patient mule and the household prepared for bed. Sam and Nellie were allowed the luxury of having the "back room" all to themselves, and with expressions of weariness they retired for the night.

The three weeks that followed were happy ones. Sam and his bride spent several nights with her parents, then stayed a while with Sam's family. A week later they returned to Nellie's home. Throughout this time she babbled happily about the home she wanted Sam to build, the children they would have, and the names they would bear. As for Sam, he was early to bed and late to rise and relished every moment of his new situation.

Then Sam's world crashed about him. Nellie's older sister came over from Hindman for a visit. She and her husband lived in the Knott County seat, and she had learned to read at the Hindman Settlement School. Her "baby sister" astounded her with news of her wedding and proudly brought the marriage license for her inspection. "You see," she said as she handed it over, "it's all legal and proper the way people are supposed to get married."

The older sister looked at the papers in astonishment. At the top of the document was a picture of an immense bull, his nostrils flaring as if at the sight of a luscious heifer. The document was the pedigree for Uriah's Jersey "calf-getter."

The other paper bore the preacher's uncertain signature and the spidery "X" marks of the bride's parents as subscribing witnesses. It certified that on the day aforesaid Samuel J. Tate, out of Robert and Elizabeth Tate, had been bred to Nellie. Her family name and lineage followed. On the line reserved for name and date of issue Sam had written, "Maybe. Don't know yet."

The Frontier

BETTY SEXTON FIELDS was a Melungeon who died at the age of ninety. The origins of the "dark people" are lost in the mists of our country's history. They are found in many parts of the Appalachians and are called by many names. In some places they are known as "Guians," in others as "Red Bones," "Ramps," "Wooly-boogers," and "Portagees." According to lingering traditions they were living deep in the hills long before the Battle of Fallen Timbers in 1794.

In any event, Betty Sexton Fields was a Melungeon whose forebear fought in the Revolution. Betty came to my office because of a neighborhood disagreement, and while she was there she told me about her great-grandmother and how a little band of settlers made their way into the headwaters of the Kentucky River "back in Indian times."

Betty said that several families came together "so they wouldn't be so lonesome" and for protection against the "savages." They left the old settlements too late in the year and passed through Pound Gap in the Pine Mountain after the leaves had turned brilliant with autumn colors. Thus they had to rely on the grain they carried on their mules, the livestock they herded before them, and such wild game as they could slay in the forests.

The families found a dry place under an arching cliff where they sheltered through the winter. They "faced up" the front with upright poles and tough bark peeled from huge chestnut trees. The place was crowded and smoky, but the pioneers were unused to worldly comforts and considered it adequate until suitable lands could be located and "marked" and cabins built. In the spring all these things would be attended to and another fall would find them snugly set up on their own puncheon floors, within chinked walls, and with "rived" white oak boards above their heads.

Then winter came on. In January the snows fell and the creeks froze hard as iron. The ground was flinty and the bitter wind zipped through deerskins and woolens like a razor. The mastfall had been light and game was scarce. The men broke the ice to fish in the water but the black bass lay deep and were not tempted by the bait. The stocks of meal and parched corn dwindled and vanished. The families became desperate. The forest was silent. The dense canebrakes in the bottoms at the creek mouths were traversed time and time again without starting deer, elk, or buffalo. Time after time the hunters returned with nothing more than a few rabbits.

At last one night the men came home beaten and hopeless. There was no game in this vast wild country or, if it existed, it was hidden beyond their ken. Weak and hungry, they sat down around the fire, resigned to starvation. They could think of no way out of their dilemma and supposed that two or three more days of gnawing hunger and piercing cold would bring the end.

While they huddled in despair, Betty's great-grandmother put a chunk of fresh wood on the fire and sat down with the hunters. She told them not to give up, that things would turn out better tomorrow. She said that when they rose the next morning she would be missing from the camp. They must load their rifles with fresh dry powder and go into the forest very early. They would find a sign marked on a beech tree and should wait there in silence. The bark would be cut with an "upside down cross," and she demonstrated in the dust: ┤ They must not leave the marked tree under any circumstance. In a little while they would see a herd of deer approaching, led by a black doe. Each hunter would aim at a deer and kill it, but they must not aim at the black doe. "No matter what happens, you must not shoot the foremost deer!" she warned them.

Dawn came with calamitous cold. Only glowing embers remained of the fire but it was stoked to desultory life with a few fallen branches from the gigantic oaks and chestnuts that encircled the "rock house." Mrs. Sexton was nowhere to be seen, and everything went as she had predicted. By the first light of dawn they found the huge regal beech, the inverted cross carved deep into its silvery bark. They waited with gnawing bellies under the twisted branches and amid the gnarled roots. About two hours after sunrise they heard a faint sound and there, moving in their direction, was a herd of a dozen deer, their heads high, their dainty hooves clicking against the crusted snow. At the head of the procession was a black doe which even the antlered bucks followed. On they came, closer and closer, wholly oblivious to the long-barreled rifles now aimed in their direction. Suddenly the black doe stopped and the others passed behind her. The black doe lowered her head as if sniffing the snow, and the rifles boomed. The black doe dashed into the forest and the others scattered amid a flurry of sharp hooves and white tails. They left behind them on the snow three carcasses—two bucks and a doe. As the men carried the heavy bodies to the half-starved camp they marveled that the herd could have escaped their relentless search during the preceding days.

The women and children were jubilant. They ran to meet the hunters and there among them was Mrs. Sexton, safely returned from her mysterious foray into the frozen forest.

The ravenous people filled their stomachs with the fresh venison and drank the fat rendered out of the intestines and other "soft parts." Their strength and spirits revived and they looked forward to spring. But the snow and bitter cold lingered and within a week the last of the meat was gone. Again they scoured the forest for game but found nothing. When they were worn out and sick with exhaustion and frustration Mrs. Sexton came again to their fire. The next morning all went precisely as before, and the hunters returned a second time laden with venison. At the camp they were greeted by the woman whose assistance had saved them from starvation. But the snow lay deep through February and the arctic winds blew with such terrible effect that the men could scarcely stir from the flames. Then came the night when the men returned empty-handed and the last morsel of the meat was gone.

Mrs. Sexton told them a third time that when they awakened she would be gone from the camp, and they must do as she had instructed them before. "Take good aim, and do not shoot the foremost deer!"

The next morning the men waited at the giant beech, puzzled by the strange happenings that had kept them alive through seven terrible weeks. One of them was named Gibson, a tall muscular man who feared nothing. His rifle carried a heavy charge of powder and two balls. When the black doe came into view he aimed at her chest and when she dipped her head he fired. The two balls struck close together and penetrated her lungs. When Gibson rushed up with his butcher knife in hand the men shivered because her dying eyes glared at him with the hatred they had seen in cornered wolves. The others berated Gibson for disobeying the instructions that had brought them so much good fortune, but he laughed at them.

This time Mrs. Sexton did not meet them at the camp. They searched far and wide for her and called her name many times. They fired their rifles and listened for some answering cry, but none came. She was never found, and no trace of her footprint was seen in the snow.

When Gibson cut up the carcass of the black doe, it gave off a foul, sickening smell. The meat could not be eaten and was discarded in a sinkhole where it was covered with brush and rocks. Eventually warm weather softened the soil, and Betty's great-grandfather buried the carcass.

Betty watched me to make sure I was listening to her story. "You see," she explained, "my great-grandmother followed the dark ways and had many powers people nowadays know nothing about. The dark ways were brought from the yon side of the waters, and my people brought them to the new settlements.

People who followed the dark ways were healthy and strong and lived long lives. They was never sick a day of their lives."

She went on with her tale. Her great-grandfather had learned many things from his wife and now he tried hard to remember all that he had heard her say and seen her do concerning her mysterious practices. He was not a witch himself but had lived with his wife for a dozen or so years, and she had told him much that he took lightly at the time but now recalled as important. He too could follow the dark ways.

Spring days melted the snow. The streams ran high with sparkling water, and wild flowers peeped up where the sun touched the forest loam. The people under the "rock house" scattered in search of lands suitable for farming, and Sexton was left with a motherless brood and grief for his vanished wife.

He went deep into the wilderness in search of things he had heard her mention. At last he found them high in a hillside cove. A gigantic poplar had fallen, leaving a hollow stump about three feet high. Lichens and fungi grew on its rotten sides, and dark, foul-smelling water filled its basin. Toadstools—"the devil's wild flowers"—grew all about, sprouting in profusion out of the prostrate trunk. A dozen yards away a white beech lifted its twisted limbs. The water-filled stump was in a little clearing which the moon could reach on a cloudless night. The setting was satisfactory.

Sexton carved an "image" into the bark of the beech tree. It was a passable outline of the face and features of Gibson, the errant hunter. That night when darkness enveloped the forest, Sexton dipped his hand into the stump water and sprinkled it over the image. Six nights in a row he returned and repeated the ritual. On the seventh night he brought a sharp wooden spike carved from seasoned hickory and hammered the "trunnel" into the living bark and wood of the beech so that it protruded from the forehead of the image. Then he went home.

A day or so later Gibson awoke with a headache. It worsened throughout the day. The next day he was frantic with pain and

97

sent for Sexton. Betty's great-grandfather reached the unfinished cabin to find the man stretched in agony on a bed of moss. He looked at Sexton and grimaced with the agony inside his skull. "You have hexed me for killing your wife," he moaned. He said he felt as if a nail had been driven straight into his forehead. Then he died.

Betty told me things that witches knew and other people did not suspect. For example, God made everything that people eat and "made it perfect." All food should be eaten whole just as it grows out of the ground. "The devil tells us to take the bran from the wheat and the peel from the apple, but the people who believe in the Lord know better." Most of the things people eat these days have been "touched by the devil," and had the best parts taken out. That is why there is so much sickness and so many doctors and hospitals.

Folks talk about vitamins, she said, and think they are something new. The people who followed the dark ways knew about them thousands of years ago and concentrated them in the potions they boiled out of forest plants. "People have to take vitamins out of a bottle," she opined, "because old Satan has been tampering with their grub!"

I asked her about the poplar stump in the clearing, and she explained. When the devil passes through the dark woods he looks for a hollow stump with water in it. He is vain, stops to see himself reflected in the moonlit water, and will come back again and again. That becomes Satan's ground.

She smiled and concluded her lecture. "The next time you go for a walk in the woods look for a hollow stump in a little clear place. If the stump is full of water and has toadstools growing on and around it you may know Satan has been there. If you are there at midnight you may see his old black face in the moonlight."

Hiram Caudill had a distinction which he shared with few Americans of the 1960s. His life and that of his father, Isham, spanned the entire history of the United States from the Articles of Confederation to his death. Isham was born before George Washington became president, and Hiram died at ninety-four in 1965, in the second year of Lyndon Johnson's presidency. Isham's father was James, who came to Cowan Creek in Letcher County in 1792. He passed the century mark before he died of "summer fever" and was buried in a coffin fashioned out of a huge linden log. Isham was the kind of man most Americans would like to be. After his family had grown up and departed he took a new bride at the age of eighty-two and begat Hiram "on her body," as the English common law judges so quaintly phrased it. Isham lasted twenty more years and told Hiram many things, some of which he passed on to me.

James was actually James, Jr. His father, James, Sr., lived in Wilkes County, North Carolina, when that new sovereignty took a census in 1784. All the multitudes who bear the name of Caudill in eastern Kentucky carry his genes. His four sons, James, Stephen, Benjamin, and Sampson, moved westward and from them are descended the "sets" or "generations."

Hiram claimed that Isham told him James, Jr., headed for the western hills in the year when Kentucky acquired statehood. In 1792 the central Appalachians were a vast wilderness of ferns, wild flowers, trees and canebrakes growing on steep hills capped with lovely cliffs and laced with sparkling creeks. This forest teemed with game. James, Jr., had been there before, in 1787, but when he found "Indian signs" in a fresh snow he returned to the old settlements rather than risk death at the hands of "savages." When he came back to stay, his son was five or six— "within the age of memory."

James came from the "old state" with his wife, children, guns, skillets, axes, bedding, and farm tools. All were conveyed on the backs of two or three pack animals and they came to a new land human cupidity had not yet marked. They followed a faint path which they knew erroneously as "Nemacolin's trace." It ran westward through the valley of Virginia and passed, like a gossamer thread, through the Pound or "Sounding" Gap in Pine Mountain. This 2,700-foot ridge parallels the Cumberland and, in those far-off times, was known variously as Great Laurel Ridge, Sandy Mountain, and Hollow Mountain. The trace led to a tangle of hills and hollows two hundred miles above the tiny village that presumed to call itself the capital of a raw new commonwealth.

Twelve miles below the gap the little party forced its way through a canebrake between hills that crowded close against the tiny river. A stream rippled in from the south, and James turned up the valley. The little caravan encountered a disgruntled hunter named John Cowan, his lean-to shelter set up amid the cane. He had accumulated bales of furs and skins and left in a huff when the settlers intruded on his solitude. He was remembered, though, and the stream is still known as Cowan Creek.

James found a wide bottom that was overgrown with the wild bamboo or cane. This was the place, he said, and they pitched their camp at the mouth of a tiny branch that meandered in from the direction of another creek other settlers would call "Kingdom Come." James has been dead for a century and a half and the last trace of his works has vanished, but the valley he settled still bears the name he set upon it.

It was in the springtime, and the family found shelter under a cliff that was black with the smoke of old Cherokee camp fires. James set his wife and children to pulling up the wild cane by the roots so the land could be planted in corn. As for himself, he took his axe and began to fell the great trees that grew out of the valley's loam. The immemorial silence was broken by the "t-chup, t-chup" of the blade as it hewed the poplar trunks into giant planks six inches thick and eighteen inches wide. As the fields greened with the first shoots of corn he notched the ends of the timbers in a "half dovetail," and the walls rose to form Letcher County's first cabin.

James was a veteran of the Kings Mountain campaign and had learned the importance of powder and shot. In those lean days he also knew the virtues of frugality. In his time thrift built America, as, in our time, waste threatens to destroy it.

One day, a year after the disgruntled Cowan took his leave,

James was splitting black walnut fence rails to enclose his fields. His helpmeet pounded the family washing with a "battling stick" behind the cabin, and Isham's brothers and sisters applied their hoes to rows of knee-high corn. James handed eleven-year-old Isham his .41-caliber rifle and a keen knife. The rifle was charged with black powder, a pinch of tow, and a round lead ball. "Here, son," he said, as he strapped the knife to the boy's waist, "take these and go kill us a fat deer."

Isham strained to carry the twelve-pound rifle up what is now known as Brashear's Branch. The sun was hot and the path was tangled with briers and grapevines. He was pleased with the important task that had been assigned to him and was proud of the five and a half feet of deadly wood and steel he cradled in his arms.

In midmorning he came to a little glade encircled by beech trees. The nuts from the previous year had sprouted and a dozen deer were grazing on the shoots. When the rifle cracked, the elated boy was delighted to see one of the fat animals spring up, then sprawl amid the heaved and twisted roots.

Isham caught the convulsing animal by its head and pushed the sharp knife into its throat, leaping back as the blood spurted in a crimson stream. When the body was still he began dragging it toward the cabin, a few feet at a time, over the rocky path. Noon had passed when the triumphant boy reached the field and called to his father. "Fresh meat," he yelled. "Come and look at it!"

His father inspected the animal. "A good shot. Right in the heart," he noted. "Well bled, too. Meat is no good unless the throat is cut in time for the heart to pump out the blood."

Then he went to the creek bank and pulled up a long stalk of the tough cane. He plucked off the leaves and swished it through the air in an appraising manner. He walked over to the puzzled boy and seized him by the arm. The cane stalk rose and fell across Isham's back, leaving streaks of fire. Again and again it was applied until the cane was splintered and useless, and Isham's shoulders were an expanse of pain.

When James released his son's arm, he said, "There, now, that will be a lesson for you! When I send you after fresh meat again, don't you waste powder and ball on a doe. The next time you make sure you bring back a big buck!"

Our pioneer ancestors were not permissive parents, and lessons seldom had to be taught twice.

Lenville Whitaker lived at Hallie near the mouth of Line Fork Creek and possessed a vast fund of tales about "settlement days." In his old age he lived alone and was grateful for visitors. He was a skilled gardener and loved to reward his friends with vegetables, melons, cushaws, and pumpkins.

Lenville told me about the hardihood and ingenuity of the frontier women. We give unstinting praise to our forefathers as hunters and Indian fighters but often overlook the tough-minded wives who bore their children and endured their every hardship.

Lenville said that his forebears came to the Line Fork country before 1800. After the cabin was built and a few acres had been cleared, his great-great-grandfather died. His demise was a calamity for the Widow Whitaker and her numerous children. The nearest neighbor was five miles away. There was no government to afford aid or protection, and Indian incursions were not out of the question. Each family had to fend for itself and survive by its own wits and labor, or perish unnoticed. There were no others to see or care.

A distant settler had a hand mill for grinding corn. When her husband had been decently buried, Mrs. Whitaker shelled a bushel of the grain and laid it on the back of her twelve-year-old son. She told him to make his way along the creek to the Kentucky River, then up the river to the mill owner's home. He must push the millstones around and around until the corn became coarse meal. The boy's twin sister went along to take turns at the mill and to "keep him company." They left home soon after dawn and should have made the fourteen-mile round trip by nightfall. They were admonished not to loiter along the way.

But darkness fell and they had not returned. Many dangers

beset the trail and she knew them all, so she made a "pine light" and went to find them. She met the burdened pair toiling along the dark trail, the boy and girl taking turns beneath the heavy meal sack. She carried her trusty axe and as they came through the hill gap at midnight the mountain lions or "pant-hers" were lying on the huge rocks above the dim track. She prepared for battle as they passed beneath the crouching beasts, but they did not spring. The cougars "gritted their teeth" and growled at the puffing trio from the crags that are still known as the "panther rocks."

Those panthers and the wolves that roamed in a pack through the cane thickets and along the hills were the bane of the widow's life. They killed her chickens and threatened her indispensable milk cow, sheep, and hogs. She resolved to get rid of them and to make the woods safe for her livestock.

She hid at a salt lick and shot a deer. She bled the carcass and left a trail of blood from the salt lick to her door. Game was scarce that December, and the hungry cats smelled the blood. She had cut a six-inch notch at the bottom of the door where the heavy oak portal rubbed against the rough sill. There she sprinkled more of the blood and laid a dripping haunch of the venison just inside. She shut the door and barred it, then waited with her axe close at hand.

The mountain lions followed the bloody trail to the lonely cabin and sniffed at the sill. They screamed about the tiny round-pole barn that sheltered the precious livestock. She heard the terrified snorting of her cow and the grunting of hogs as the predators clawed at them through the cracks. Then the cats padded back to her door and their red tongues licked at the tantalizing blood and meat.

Frustrated and empty, they leaped onto the white-oak boards of the roof, but the timbers held. They clawed at the single shuttered window, but the wooden hinges were unyielding. Back they crept to the door and that tempting notch beyond which lay the succulent flesh. Their hot breath swept in, rank with the stench of carrion from the meat rotting between their teeth. Sud-

103

denly a huge tawny paw streaked in to seize the venison and the waiting axe flashed down. The severed foot with its razor-sharp talons was flung aside. The hideous screams of the carnivore and the hot blood from its spouting arteries brought the others to the same deadly experiment. One after the other the creatures left a forepaw on the puncheon floor.

The widow waited two days, and then took her axe and skinning knife to the panther rocks. Some of her victims were already dead from loss of blood, and the remorseless axe crashed down on the skulls of the others. She skinned out the carcasses and tanned the hides. They made warm, soft bed covers against the cold winds that slipped past the chinking between the logs.

"She treated the wolves the same way," Lenville concluded. "She cleaned out the whole pack and used their skins to make floor rugs."

He showed me where her vanished cabin had stood. "I am proud to be descended from a woman like that," he said.

Jont Cornett lived across the hill from Lenville on Turkey Creek. When he was eighty-nine he told me how Defeated Creek acquired its unusual name.

Jont was a descendant of William Cornett, who came to the hills with Gideon Ison and Gudgeon Ingram first as a hunter, then as a settler. On their first hunting foray these three were accompanied by three others from the "old settlements." Their names were lost to Jont, but their dust lies somewhere along that obscure creek which they named by their dying.

On a September morning about 1785 the little band rose early to look for buffalo in the canebrakes. They turned up a stream but saw only "old signs" of the shaggy beasts. They saw something else, however—the smoke of a camp fire. Cornett volunteered to spy out the area and report back about the fire and the people who had kindled it. The hunters suspected that they were Indians at breakfast.

He entered the canebrake with his long rifle at the ready and was back within half an hour. The people at the fire were Indians, seven of them, cooking wild turkeys for their morning meal. If the white hunters could creep up stealthily they could fire before they were observed. With luck they might kill the whole bunch of "red-skinned varmints" and take their scalps for trophies. Then they could have those broiled turkeys for themselves!

A plan was discussed and agreed upon and the white hunters slunk toward the unsuspecting "savages." A few moments later, though, they were struck by a fusillade from the thick cane and the Choctaw war whoop shattered the morning quiet. Cornett, Ison, and Ingram escaped the valley and fled southward, but their friends were not so lucky. Brought down by the Indian bullets, they were butchered and scalped. The remaining whites were pursued closely as they ran downstream and hid in a laurel thicket from which they hoped to spring an ambush of their own. But the Choctaws were too wary to give them a second chance, and the dead remained unavenged victims of the border wars.

"So you can see how treacherous the Indians was," Jont summed up. "They knowed the white men was there and made that smoke and cooked them turkeys just to git their attention. They let on that they didn't suspicion a thing. They figured the whites would do exactly what they did and set up that devilish ambush for them."

He reflected on the sins and shortcomings of Indians. "Yes, sir, it's just like the old people used to say. You just couldn't trust Indians 'cause they would bushwhack the white folks every time they got a chance."

"Anyway, that is where our forefathers was defeated and had to run away, and it has been called the Defeated Creek ever since."

The frontier outlook died slowly in the hills. County Judge George Wooten of Leslie County and I once discussed the isolated pockets of extreme social lag found here and there. He asked me to accompany him on an expedition to a place near Devil's Jump where we met a family that could have walked out

105

of the Appalachian frontier of 1775. The man, woman, and brood of children lived in a one-room round-pole cabin roofed with split boards of whiteoak. The cracks were chinked with clay, and the floor was the barren earth. The shelter was no more than five and a half feet high and had no window. Even more striking, there was no chimney. A fire was maintained on a circle of stones in the middle of the room with the smoke drifting out a "smoke hole" in the roof. The only manufactured items I saw in that primitive hut were a skillet and a single-barrel Stevens shotgun. The rest was homemade after the fashion of the first settlers. The crops in the nearby garden were beans, corn, potatoes, onions, and cabbage—the backwoods staples. There was a row of tobacco for the pipes and for chewing. A wooden keg of moonshine was visible. A coonskin was drying on a rack. It was as if we had dropped in for a chat with settlers on the Holston River or the Cumberland Trail in the days of Daniel Boone and Simon Kenton.

The judge showed me the sign on the nearby church. Reflecting the hard-scrabble names so often found in the hills, as well as the fundamentalist old-time religion, it read, "Hell-for-Certain Regular Baptist Church."

Wilson Fields was a lawyer who had the good sense to quit the practice when he was about fifty. He introduced me to Choctaw Ingram and Choctaw introduced me to the memorable sound of the Choctaw war whoop.

My father, Wilson, and I were driving along Line Fork Creek on what passed for a road in 1940. We met Choctaw walking homeward with a bag of flour on his shoulder. Choctaw was a half-breed and his Choctaw blood was prominent in his coppery skin, arched nose, and high cheek bones. Wilson's grandfather was an Indian also, and he and Choctaw were related. We stopped and exchanged pleasantries.

Choctaw's cheek was loaded with the golden leaf. He was about eighty and had never known sickness, he said. When his joints ached he got a little dried hemp and smoked it. Hemp smoke, he said, was a mighty fine remedy.

Wilson told him that I was a young man who had heard people talk about the war whoop and would be mighty pleased if Choctaw would sound the cry that had once terrified the enemies of his people. Choctaw "hunkered down" by the side of the road and chewed and spat. Finally he said he needed a dram first. Wilson went to his battered Oldsmobile and came back with a quart jar of the stuff our friend and host Jarrett Lewis had bestowed upon us that morning. Jarrett kept only the best, and Choctaw sniffed it with approval. He swallowed a long drink, then rested and chewed some more. Wilson said Choctaw was the only Indian left who could sound the war whoop, and he had also learned the rebel yell from John Holcomb who had fought "clear through from start to finish."

Choctaw took another pull at the fruit jar. "This is the war whoop," he said. Suddenly he drew in a deep breath and from his throat came the most startling sound I have ever heard—a high, bloodcurdling shriek that dropped to lower volumes and different scales of weirdness as the pent-up breath was expended. It expired with a series of hideous grunts.

The sound left me thoroughly impressed. Then he filled his lungs again and emitted a shrill cry that sounded much like the drawn-out wailing bark of a hyena. It was a sound full of hatred, derision, scorn and defiance. This was the rebel yell.

Neither of the cries can be properly described, and I certainly could not begin to duplicate them. Their impact on an enemy must have been terrifying when they came from a thicket at the beginning of a battle charge.

Choctaw opened his shirt front and stuck the fruit jar inside. Without another word he shouldered his flour sack and strode on, leaving Wilson and my father speechless at the loss of their "dram." Other creatures, though, made up for their lack of protest. On a hillside pasture cows bawled, and at a house a hundred yards away a couple of hounds howled in sympathy and wonderment. Their owner threw a rock at them and ordered them to shut up. We heard him grumbling with much profanity that he had never heard "such a God-damned racket" in his life. His wife came out of the house to suggest in a worried voice that somebody was in trouble. "Trouble, hell," he rejoined, "whoever hollered that way is bound to be out of his trouble. Yells like that would kill the Holy Ghost!"

Francesca Monjiardo

FRANCESCA MONJIARDO was born in a village in southern Italy, in the Campania, and came to America in 1902. He passed through the immigration proceedings at Ellis Island and went to West Virginia where he and his younger brother, Dominic, built commissaries and railroad bridges. Then he heard that railroads were being built up the Cumberland, the Big Sandy, and the Kentucky rivers in eastern Kentucky to open an immense new coalfield. These streams had to be crossed scores of times with steel bridges set on stone piers and abutments. Francesca Monjiardo knew how to carve stones and cement them together in bonds that would never give way. He came to Kentucky to "work on the railroads" and stayed there, a productive and exemplary citizen, until his death in 1963.

When I built my home in 1948 he laid the foundation. He and Dominic went to bedrock before they poured the steel-reinforced "footer." Dominic knew only a few words of English and used them to reassure me. "We do good job," he grinned. They did just that and everything they constructed for me is solid, staunch, and perfect to this day. The Monjiardos built for the centuries.

Francesca was not known by that name among his neighbors. Over the years his name changed and was Americanized. The first name became Frank. His last name became Monjardi, then Majority. For a half century he was Frank Majority. It was easier that way and a lot simpler.

Frank loved to play checkers with my colleague at the bar, Le-Roy Fields. In Frank's last years ill health compelled him to lay aside his tools, and almost every afternoon at four o'clock he dropped by Mr. Fields's office for an hour of deep concentration over the red and black discs. They invariably separated with vows to resume the contest on the following day. Each day's victor was immensely pleased with his triumph. Sometimes Frank would stop at my office afterward to tell me a story.

Whitesburg had a considerable Italian community. Most of them came from Naples or the village of San Andrea where, since the days of Nero and the martyrs, the Roman Catholic Church held unchallenged sway. Not one of them had seen a member of any other church before they sailed for America. All were superb workmen, and they left the country an enduring legacy of piers and bridges, concrete streets, stone retaining walls, homes, commercial buildings and churches. The town of Hindman is largely their work, the old part of it being simply a southern Italian village serving as an eastern Kentucky county seat.

In Whitesburg two of the immigrants built hillside houses of massive cut-stone construction, with flights of stairs and gray stone pillars, which look for all the world as if they had been plucked from San Andrea itself and set down in new hills an ocean to the west. Along "Tally Street" on College Hill on dewy mornings the gardens glistened with rows of succulent celery, onions, garlic, leeks, potatoes, rutabagas, tomatoes, cabbages, peppers, and eggplants. In the afternoons the street reverberated with the shouts of children in a strange mixed tongue compounded of the dialect of the Campania and the ancient slow English speech of the Appalachian Highlands.

Frank told me how some Italians made their way to the Kentucky hills. He emphasized that he did not "come over" in any such fashion but that whole shiploads of his contemporaries got to the new world in precisely that way.

According to Frank times were very hard in southern Italy early in the century. The streets teemed with youths for whom there was absolutely no employment. Agricultural lands had been cut up into tiny farms intensively worked by the owners

110

and their children. There was little industry and practically no construction. In their idleness the youths turned to mischief and petty crime. The carabinieri locked them up and the judges tried them, but the prisons could not contain their endless numbers. America, he said, was an excellent alternative to jail.

He described the experiences of a friend. The friend was in jail in Naples, having been charged, tried, and convicted. The jails were so packed that there was scarcely standing room. One day the prisoners were brought into a courtroom under guard, the vigilant carabinieri with their short rifles posted at each door and stairwell. A judge explained the facts of life. They had all been convicted, but as yet their sentences had not been formally imposed. Officially they were still without criminal records. A United States Steel Corporation ship was in the harbor, and labor agents were recruiting workers for mills and mines. All who wanted to do so could immigrate. The rest would go to prison. The judge asked for a show of hands and all but three or four voted for the New World.

Desks were set up just outside the doors. The men filed out one by one, answering the questions that would be put to them at Ellis Island. Then the watchful policemen herded them to the docks where steam launches conveyed them to the ship. When the vessel was packed it drew off from the shore so none could escape and swim back to land. Ten days later they arrived in New York.

There they went through the inevitable processing—questions were answered, chests were listened to, throats were looked at, records were scrutinized and stamped. Then they were put ashore at what is now Battery Park. Lines of "New York's finest" and a contingent of Pinkerton agents saw them safely aboard a waiting train. When each seat was taken and a few of the new Americans were parked in the aisles, the doors were locked and the Pinkerton men took up positions to prevent escapes en route. The windows were covered with dark green paint to prevent the newcomers from seeing the towns and countryside through which they were passing. A few days later the stiff and sleepy immigrants stepped off the cars at a raw new mining town called Lynch, Kentucky.

There they were "processed" again. Each "transportation man" was given a bill for his ship and railroad fares, including the ghastly food he had eaten. All of it was totaled and the sum was impressive. Wages amounted to fifteen cents per hour and years of work would be required before the debt could be worked off. In the meantime the men were assigned places in the huge boardinghouses and issued shovels, carbide lamps, and work clothes. These costs, too, went onto the bill, and the men went to the mines.

The United States Coal and Coke Company kept "rousters" whose job it was to see that the new Americans arrived on time and worked full shifts six days weekly. If one drank too much or suffered from the blues and stayed in bed, the "rousters would get him." These well-armed and muscular characters traveled in pairs, and they simply dragged the idler from his bed, slapped him into wakefulness, pounded him into his work clothes, and escorted him to the mine where a "man-car" whisked him underground. His instructions were explicit. "You Wop son-of-a-bitch, get in there and work! You've got a contract to pay off!"

If a man worked poorly or was lazy, the rousters would back him against a wall, detail his shortcomings, and give him a good drubbing. Thus the mine masters maintained discipline in the southern hills.

The Italians were diligent and hardworking. Within a few years the company was paid off and sweethearts were imported from Italy. Nearly all of them left the camps and mining for construction jobs and their own homes. Nearly all did well. Some got rich. A few took their savings and returned to Italy where they were pauperized again by World War II.

The war brought hardships and inconveniences to my good friend Frank Majority. He used to tell me about them, shaking his head with a mixture of disbelief and good humor.

A few weeks after Pearl Harbor, I was in a barbershop at Whitesburg while Frank was being shaved of the tough whiskers

112

that grew on his redoubtable Campanian chin. One of the waiting customers recommended that all Japanese, Italians, and Germans in the United States be "shipped home" and shot down "like dogs" if they tried to come back. This brought Frank to a sitting position, his face soapy, his eyes wrathful, and his arms going like a windmill. "Now, that's a helluva way to talk!" he roared. "When the Eye-talians comma to thissa country here, he havva no bridge, no street, no house excepta old log house. When you wanta crossa creek you jumpa from one rock to another rock lika monkey. Don't hava nothin', don't know nothin', don't do nothin'. We Eye-talians builda the bridge, builda the street, builda the houses, builda the towns. Get everthinga fix upa good and show others how to builda things, then America say 'You go back where you comma from, don't awant you anymore!'"

The loudmouth departed unshorn, and the barber went back to work on Frank's whiskers, interrupted by occasional indignant eruptions from his customer.

As the European war spread and intensified, our Italian friends in their little colony at the head of the Kentucky River had numerous tribulations thrust upon them. For example, Mussolini's invasion of tiny Albania triggered a major crisis in their peaceful affairs. The town's principal eating place was a small restaurant called the Coney Island Cafe, operated by Tom John, the only Albanian who ever ventured into those parts. A large round table stood near the entrance of the Coney Island and the Italians gathered at it nightly to gossip and, after repeal, to drink glasses of wine. About seven-thirty Tom invariably set an immense glass bowl in the middle of the table, a bowl brimming with freshly cut and lightly tossed lettuce, peppers, celery, green onions, bits of garlic, shreds of carrot, anchovies, and pieces of hard, dry salami. This mixture was dressed with olive oil, salt, and an abundance of black pepper. Slices of Italian bread, toasted and brushed with garlic butter, went down with the vino and salad. For an hour there was relaxation with the food and drink, cigarettes and pipes, soft talk of jobs and women, and of youthful days in the grape and olive groves of Italy. For a decade their evening ritual went peacefully and happily.

Then one day the morning newspaper informed Tom John that Mussolini's legions had crossed the borders of Albania and King Zog had fled the country. Throughout the day the radio kept Tom posted on the progress of the invaders. Then came evening and the chattering Italians. The action of the Italian army was uppermost in their conversation, and its implications were discussed with much excited arm waving. Charlie Voci was expansive and mellow. "No can beat Mussolini," he told a customer who was devouring one of Tom's hamburgers. "Too beeg, too strong!"

At this Albania counterattacked. There would be no more crisp salads, buttered toast, or vino, no more pleasant chatter and pensive songs on these premises! Tom charged out of the kitchen, removing his apron as he advanced. He bore down on the Calabrians, his black eyes flashing, his bristly eyebrows and mustache arched and curled in anger. He waved the apron like a bullfighter's cape, after the manner of a farmer's wife herding her chickens or sheep. Before the flapping of the not overly clean garment the Italians quailed, gave ground, and fled. "Out!" Tom shouted. "Out! All out! Your country invade my country! You no come here anymore!" He followed them onto the street to warn of dire consequences if they should ever again enter the Coney Island Cafe. Disconsolate and roofless, they scattered to their homes to plot a diplomatic initiative aimed at restoration of peace, harmony, and the old comfortable order.

Frank and his friends built the beautiful little Methodist Church at Whitesburg, surely one of the finest examples of the stonecutters' skill to be found in Kentucky. The Presbyterian Church was constructed during the hard depression years of the 1930s and these men contributed many hundreds of hours of highly skilled free labor to its foundations and walls. There was no Catholic church in the community and several of them regularly attended the Presbyterian services. Frank was there almost every Sunday for many years and was one of the organizers of the men's Bible class. He attended so long and so regularly that the entire community thought of him as a Presbyterian. He was for a long time a member of the building committee.

When the walls were going up, Frank and Joe Romeo quarried a huge slender stone on which they worked with infinite care. Blow by blow their chisels produced an unusual shape—the leg, foot, and heel of the map of Italy. Their friends contributed a perfecting tap here and there, and the upright shape was incorporated into the masonry just to the right of the front door. The Italians brought some wine with them and scandalized the Presbyterians by toasting "the old country" when the stone was cemented into its place.

After Pearl Harbor the congregation remembered that stone and the fact that Mussolini had declared war against the United States. At their bidding a native-born stonecutter carved the map of Italy to pieces. The stone can still be traced if one takes the trouble, but the offending shape was so reduced and defaced that it ceased to annoy the patriotic Calvinists.

Frank's son Jim was a marine fighting his way across the Pacific in the island-hopping campaign toward Tokyo. He shocked and scandalized his father after the battle of Iwo Jima. His letter said that a present was on the way, something to help Frank in his pipe-smoking. The package arrived, a heavy box stoutly tied with string and wrapped with brown paper much tattered from rough handling by the military postal service. Frank dashed home to open it in the presence of Jim's mother. The strings were cut away, the paper removed, the lid of the box lifted, and the loving parents stared in disbelief at the contents. Frank's work-roughened hands lifted out a human skull, its base fastened to a square of coconut wood, its teeth grinning in a ghastly grimace. His affectionate son had made him a pipe holder out of the bleached skull of a dead Japanese soldier!

Frank dropped his other work for the next few days and devoted all of his attention to the problem this new arrival had thrust upon him. He acquired a walnut plank, planed and smoothed it, and shaped it into a tiny coffin which he padded with cotton and lined with a soft white cloth. In this receptacle he deposited the desecrated skull. No one else wanted to attend a funeral for a "dead Jap," so Frank sat in reverent silence praying for the soul of the fallen soldier. He tucked the box under his arm and carried it to a little flat on a hillside overlooking Whitesburg and buried it. The depth was proper too, a good six feet. Then Frank carved out a stone slab and set it up to give notice that one of God's children sleeps below.

Frank told me about his brushes with the law, his close calls, and narrow escapes. Out of these experiences he developed a whole hearted determination to live within the statutes.

Frank owned a few acres of hillside land which he terraced after the manner of his ancestors in San Andrea. There he planted vines, which he trimmed and manured for crops of delicious plump grapes. These were crushed and the juice was fermented into good red vino. The vino added zest to meals and elevated spirits when thoughts turned to faraway villages and lost friends and kinsmen.

Then came Prohibition and the Volstead Act. Frank and his friends from Naples and San Andrea continued to grow their grapes, make their wine, and drink it as the spirit moved them. They even gave some of it away to appreciative visitors, as a result whereof Frank found himself in United States District Court at Pikeville charged with the offense of manufacturing vinous beverages and disposing of them in violation of law. Judge Cochran heard Frank's explanation, looked at the reports on the offender, and let Frank go home unpunished. But he lectured him on his duties as a citizen. "You must obey the laws," he admonished. "Congress has outlawed the manufacture and distribution of vinous spirits. You must heed that law irrespective of any customs you may have acquired as a young man in your native land."

Frank went away chastened and penitent.

Years passed and bombs fell on Pearl Harbor. A few weeks later Frank saw an official notice in the post office. It warned all "enemy aliens" to register forthwith at the nearest office of the Naturalization Service, using forms to be obtained from the postmaster. "Enemy aliens" included Italians who had not been naturalized, and Frank had never gone to the trouble to obtain his citizenship papers. He had seen little need to do so. The likelihood of a war between Uncle Sam and Italy seemed slight, and the Letcher County election officials never challenged his right to vote. He owned his home, had married an American woman from Big Cowan Creek, and had four children born under the red, white, and blue. What more was needed?

But Frank was warned that the penalty for failing to register was a ten-year prison sentence, plus a fine of $10,000. He got the forms and had his daughter fill them out that very night. The next day they were mailed and Frank breathed easier. The days and months passed, battles were fought, and the war entered its final phase. Then the marshals came for Frank. He wound up in that same grim courtroom a second time—charged now with the offense of registering under an alias. Francesca Monjiardo had stated his name as Frank Majority, "in violation of statutes in such cases made and provided."

As he had to Judge Cochran, Frank now explained to his successor. He had come from Italy forty-two years ago, had worked at many jobs to improve the country, had married an American woman, and raised four children, all of whom were born in this country, and had sent two sons to war. Ministers stood up to give testimonials for his good character. As to the name, he had been called Frank Majority so long that he had simply forgotten the old-world name that had been applied to him at a christening in the little church of San Andrea. He had meant no wrong, no offense, no illegality. He stood repentant, confessed, reformed.

The judge might have dismissed the charge and forgotten about it without further ado. He did dismiss it, of course, but first he felt compelled to exercise the judicial urge to pontificate and lecture. He told Frank about the greatness of America and of our duty to uphold that greatness, and to be good citizens. We must obey the laws, cheerfully and to the letter. He reminded

117

Frank that he had been there before as a violator of the laws of his adopted country. The next time the full penalty might be exacted. "Go now," he said, "but be more careful in the future."

Frank went, reflecting on the difficulties of avoiding pitfalls in a land that remained alien in spite of all he could do to learn its ways.

Back home, inspired by the new chance the judge had so kindly granted him, Frank went about the business of helping America achieve victory. He needed coal for his stove and it was hard to come by even in the coalfields in that last year of the war. The Solid Fuels Administration decreed that nearly all of it should be shipped to war industries, leaving little for the home front. A thin vein outcropped near Frank's little house and he decided to dig enough of it to supply his own needs and perhaps those of Dominic and the Polichettis. He dug away the dirt with a mattock and shovel, and then loosened wheelbarrow loads with a pick. This simple operation satisfied his fuel requirements and provided a bit of heat to one or two of his old San Andrea neighbors as well.

Then came another upsetting trip to the post office. There plain for all men to see was another notice directed to the attention of any "person, firm, or corporation engaged directly or indirectly in the production of coal." Such person, firm, or corporation was warned to register with the Solid Fuels Administration and receive a code number. The SFA would then allocate his output to eligible war industries at prices fixed by the Office of Price Administration. Numerous terrifying statutes were cited. The penalty for failing to comply was that same dreadful combination: ten years imprisonment or a $10,000 fine, or both. The application forms could be obtained from the postmaster.

He demanded the forms and the postmaster said he didn't need them, that Frank's trifling house-coal digging was not covered by the statute.

But he was adamant. "I been indict twice, I not be indict again," he vowed.

He would also make certain that the form was properly executed. He carried it to his checker-playing friend, LeRoy Fields, to be properly filled in and sworn to. Fields tried to dissuade him. "The government doesn't want to know about your little wheelbarrow operation for your own stove," he explained.

But Frank knew better. That notice covered *every* person who produced *any* coal. He would not go a third time to the prisoner's dock at Pikeville. The numerous questions were answered, insofar as answers were possible from Frank's minuscule operation. This meek mouse of free enterprise promptly aroused an obstreperous lion of bureaucracy. Frank was inundated by mail, all of it in sturdy manila envelopes containing gigantic questionnaires. The SFA demanded to know the name of the deposit he was mining, its chemical analysis, the number of tons produced daily, the name of the railroad company servicing his operation, and so on. It directed him to ship his entire output to Dayton Power & Light Company.

Another questionnaire arrived from OPA. It wanted the same information as to the coal vein and its analysis, plus information on the number of employees, their wage per hour, day, and week, and a listing of all his expenses. In due time he was notified that he could charge $3.85 per ton.

Other forms arrived. How much electricity was he consuming? List all rubber-tired vehicles, stating whether diesel- or gasoline-powered. Name all employees, listing their addresses and the nature of services rendered. List all employees with specific production skills on Schedule H. List names and addresses of all customers, tonnage sold to each, price charged per ton, and date of each shipment. State probable production for each month in the coming year.

Each communication carried that same grim warning about ten years and $10,000.

Then came a letter from Dayton Power & Light Company demanding to know what had become of its coal. This was followed by a threat from SFA: he must ship to the "designated war industry" or face prosecution. A questionnaire a quarter of an inch thick was enclosed for his immediate attention.

Frank was frantic and Fields was overwhelmed. The little coal pit was abandoned and the stove ran short. He could not earn wages or visit his neighbors. All his energies were devoted to answering questions. Letters of explanation went forward to SFA but the torrent could not be stopped. In one day he received "eight poundsa questions." At this point Frank gave up and quit. "I justa serva the time, but I no answer the questions. Ten years onna rocka pile is better thanna ten years answer the questions!"

A year later the bureaucracies and Dayton Power & Light were still vainly bombarding Frank with inquiries.

A few months before his death Frank learned that he suffered from cancer. Dust from countless chisels had penetrated his lungs causing irritation and cell mutations. The works of his hands were visible in a score of towns—in immovable walls, in stone and concrete spans over creeks and rivers, in schools, churches, and homes. All were built to the timeless standards of ancient, imperishable Italy. His works would outlast the republic and might even be intact when the race expires, but Frank himself must die.

Frank, the faithful Presbyterian, thought the matter over carefully. He remembered the bright blue skies and the vineyards and groves he would not see again, and a church with roots so old they could not be traced—a church that, since time immemorial, had consoled peasant, prince, and pope alike. He hired a taxi to take him to Lynch, twenty-five miles away. That coal town had a Roman Catholic church and a priest. He made peace with the Church, and the young priest called the old penitent "My son." Frank confessed such minor sins as his long and work-filled life had generated. He went back to Lynch several times after that, and the priest drove across the Pine Mountain to visit Frank at his home. He died in the bosom of Holy Church.

In his last visit to my office he explained why all of this was necessary.

He had worked hard for the Presbyterians and enjoyed their

services immensely. He had been faithful in his attendance for many years and had tried to live by Presbyterian principles and teachings. But now he was old and sick. He was going to die. That is the reason he had gone to the priest.

"Getting ready to die," said Frank, "is too important to handle through the Presbyterians!"

The Straight Shooter

FESS WHITAKER was born in 1880, one of a brood of six boys and two girls. In 1918 he published his autobiography, the *History of Corporal Fess Whitaker*, which chronicled the events of his life to the grand old age of thirty-eight. The opening lines of his preface summarized his achievements: "Among the people of Letcher County no other man has so remarkable a history as Fess Whitaker; none other is so well worthy of being carefully studied by all who find pleasure in the past history and particularly by Letcher's own people. In the winning of friends he stands first; in the upbuilding of the county his influence has been strongly exerted; as a soldier on the battlefield he stands firm."

In his "history" Fess had many tales to tell. Fred and Fess, Gid and Jim, and Little and Less were the brothers. Fred left home early, and their father died when Fess was six. The task of bringing up the five remaining sons devolved onto the dauntless mother. They tried her patience, Christianity, and motherly love. One day they climbed into a mulberry tree to pick the ripe fruit, whereupon Fess began to shake the tree, with dire results when the boys fell out. "Less got two ribs broken, Little threw his left arm out of place, Gid broke his left leg, and Jim got his tailbone broke." Fess himself wound up with a fractured left thigh, and summed up the situation: "That was an awful sight, to see five brothers broke up like we were."

There was not a doctor within forty miles so his mother made splints for the damaged limbs. The splints were made of oak lumber six inches wide and the fractures healed in thirty-three days, Fess wrote.

Fess described his mother's stern mode of seeing that he learned in school. She told him that if he was unable to solve the arithmetic problems she would whip him. At the end of two weeks the numbers were still a mystery, so his mother was ready with a collection of oak limbs. Fess "played off crazy" and escaped for the moment but when the next week came to its end he still could not work the problems. His mother beat him for a while, then rested and handed him the pencil and paper. When the mysteries of mathematics still eluded him, the thrashing was renewed. After several limbs had been worn out, the answer "jumped" into his head "like a falling star." He wrote, "From that time until the present date I challenge the State of Kentucky in the arithmetic."

Fess described his early boyhood in a noteworthy paragraph:

I never spoke a word until I was nine years old. I only clucked and motioned for what I wanted. Lots of people thought I was an idiot because I could not talk. I may have looked like one, for I was a little old country boy that never cut my hair in those days only about twice a year, and I wore a big checked cotton shirt and old jean pants made by my mother, and old yarn socks, and 70-cent stogie shoes with brass toes. This was my winter suit and my summer suit was only a big yellow factory shirt and no hat or shoes.

Fess served in the army for a while after the Spanish-American War began. Then he worked for the Santa Fe Railroad Company for nine years, achieving the much-coveted position of a locomotive engineer. But the call of the hills was in his blood and he returned to Kentucky to mine coal. A few years later a summons to "public service" stirred his soul and he ran for circuit court clerk in 1911. He was narrowly defeated in a race against a strong incumbent, but he learned lessons that made him a certain winner in subsequent contests.

Fess was born in Knott County—a bastion of Democratic strength. He grew up in Letcher where the great majority of the people were Republicans. Expedience required a switch to the Grand Old Party and he explained his conversion to a large gathering of dubious Republicans. It seemed that after his father died, his mother kept two cows, "Whitey" and "Blackey." They gave plenty of milk for the family, and each year they bore calves which his mother sold. The money was used to buy shoes and clothes for her little ones. This went on with dependable regularity for several years. Then the Democrat Cleveland was elected and trouble began. Whitey and Blackey would not let a bull approach them, so there were no calves, and likewise no milk. The family suffered terribly until Cleveland fell from grace. When a Republican returned to the White House the cows "changed their tune." They chased the bull and caught him, too. There were calves for sale, and plenty of milk and butter. Therefore, Fess declared, he switched parties and became a devoted Republican.

The Republicans were not dubious for long. Fess began a winning streak that lasted thirty years. After two decades of lesser offices he was elected jailer in 1917 and continued in public office until his death ten years later. So great had his influence become by that time that his widow was twice elected his successor. When she retired, Jim Stamper ran as "Fess Whitaker's brother-in-law" and was mandated by the people to continue the good work Fess had begun. Fess had, in effect, turned the jailer's office into a hereditary fiefdom.

Fess's brother Jim operated a sawmill when I began the practice of law. He was my client for several years and told me many stories about his irrepressible brother. "Sawloggin' Jim" described a speech Fess made to a huge crowd at Whitesburg in the momentous year of 1917.

Fess believed—as do most successful politicians—that a devotion to the truth should not be allowed to interfere with one's career. Consequently he allowed himself some leeway in describing his contribution to America's victory over the treacherous Spaniards.

Fess described the Battle of San Juan Hill. It was a terrible battle indeed. The Spaniards were armed with fine Mauser rifles and wrought bloody havoc among the Americans. Fess was a Rough Rider and the battle appeared lost until that famous cavalry charge began. As all students of those memorable days are aware, the Spaniards broke and fled before the intrepid American horsemen. Swords and pistols in hand the Rough Riders routed the Spanish infantry and won a magnificent victory.

As the Spaniards retreated, the exultant Corporal Whitaker dropped down behind a stone wall to recover his breath and get off a few shots at the routed enemy from his Krag-Jorgensen rifle. As he lay there, smoke-begrimed but victorious, a large man plopped to the ground beside him. When Fess turned to look, lo and behold, it was his "old war comrade" Teddy Roosevelt. According to Jim his brother claimed that the following dialogue ensued.

> *Teddy:* We have won a great victory for our country today, Fess. One of us will be elected president because of it.
>
> *Fess:* That is true. If you are nominated I will support you with all my heart, and if I am nominated I know you will be for me!

The two warriors shook hands on the proposition there behind the shattered wall amid the swirling gunsmoke, while the sounds of popping rifles and booming cannons assailed their ears.

Time passed, Fess continued. Teddy was from the North where most of the people live, so he got the nomination. Fess did all he could to elect his old "war buddy." Teddy made a great president and all Americans were proud of him.

Then Fess decided to seek public office in his own right. He pulled a paper from his pocket and waved it in the air. It was, he affirmed, a letter from Teddy. The ex-president had learned of

Fess's political yearnings and had written to say, "Fess, it is your time to run for president and I am for you all the way."

He shook the paper at his enthralled listeners and returned it to his inner coat pocket. Then he brought the people to their feet whooping and cheering for the heroic ex-corporal. "I wrote back," he yelled, "and told my old friend Teddy that I don't want to be president of the United States, I just want to be jailer of Letcher County!"

Fess won, of course, and entered upon the high duties of that illustrious office.

Fess was a superb jailer. His "trusties" kept the courthouse scrupulously clean and his wife, Manty, fed the prisoners abundantly. Her hot biscuits were huge and tasty, and were served alongside mounds of potatoes, beans, and "hog meat." The prisoners went forth to sing the jailer's praises and to spread his renown to the outermost limits of the county. To the "jail birds" good food was the factor that separated "good old country boys" from run-of-the-mill politicians. Fess was definitely a "good old country boy."

Young Sam Collins was county judge at that time, and at first all went well. Then relationships became strained. Sam was a teetotaler while Fess—the soldier, railroader, and miner—loved to drink the moonshine whiskey that had brought renown to the hills. The judge lectured the jailer on the virtues of sobriety. The jailer told the judge about the glories of drink. Neither convinced the other, and a head-on collision became inevitable when the jailer came into the courtroom inebriated. In this condition Fess conducted the sober prisoners before the judge to be tried for public drunkenness. At this the judge made a fatal mistake and became exceedingly irate.

Judge Collins told the sheriff to arrest the jailer. The "Arm of the Court" promptly obeyed and the unsteady Fess stood before the stern protector of public morality, who sentenced Fess to jail, and then deputized Manty to see that her husband stayed shut up in those grim confines.

Fess recognized a splendid opportunity when he saw one.

126

Sam was not running for reelection in that postwar year of 1921 but was supporting a young veteran, Steve Combs, for the county's highest office. Steve was a lawyer and the very essence of probity. Hence he was vulnerable, and the jailed jailer struck.

From his bleak cell at the front of the jail Fess announced that he was a candidate for county judge. The weekly *Mountain Eagle* carried his message to the outermost precincts and the battle was joined. Fess Whitaker, the champion of the common people, was unjustly imprisoned. His political enemies had locked him up, but they could not shut him up. Fess would speak to such crowds as might gather before the county's model prison.

The crowds came and Fess spoke to them much as Huey Long might have done in Louisiana a decade later. He told them about the war and Teddy Roosevelt and the county's spic-and-span jail. He detailed the iniquities of Judge Sam Collins and the "pitiful" shortcomings of his "hand-picked candidate." He poured vitriol and ridicule on their heads, and the crowds grew.

One day a multitude assembled to hear Fess "speak to the people." Judge Collins was worried and went through the throngs to make his peace with the errant jailer. Manty jangled the huge keys as she opened the gate in the high iron fence, then the doors to the "keep" itself, and allowed His Honor to enter.

The judge asked Fess for a conference and they sat down at the dinner table. Sam told Fess he was ruining the party. Fess could not win, of course, but his assaults might weaken the GOP so that a Democrat would capture the judgeship. Drop out of the judge's race, he urged, and run again for jailer. Sam and Steve would support him and there would be victory for all. Steve would be judge, Fess would be jailer, the GOP would triumph from one end of the county to the other.

Fess said nothing. He pondered the huge crowd outside the jail and the tidings they might carry to every hill and hollow.

There was a gallon pitcher of buttermilk on the table and Fess picked it up. "Sam," he announced in tones of flat finality, "I am going to pour this buttermilk all over you!"

127

Sam jumped up and fled, with Fess in hot pursuit. The county's judge and chief executive officer ran through the iron-encased doorway pursued by the pitcher-bearing jailer. The astonished people stared and laughed. At the gate that enclosed the stone dungeon, the judge halted, his way barred. Outside were hundreds of voters; behind him was the avenging Fess. Manty was coming with the keys, but still afar off. Sam attempted to plead with the jailer to forget vengeance and put aside the pitcher of buttermilk, but Fess was implacable.

The judge cowered at the mighty gate as Fess's voice rose in tones of doom. "John the Baptist baptized with water and Jesus Christ baptized with the Holy Ghost," intoned the hero of Santiago and San Juan, "but I am going to baptize you with buttermilk!"

Thereupon he towered above Collins like a high priest at some holy rite and poured forth a generous libation of buttermilk upon the judge's pate, shoulders, and other parts. The crowd roared with glee as the triumphant jailer danced about the drenched and fallen judge. Manty opened the gate and the judge fled, derision and political doom resounding in his ears. Then Manty reclosed the gate and Fess made a speech.

Sam had come to pressure him into quitting the race, he said, but he would never betray the people. All the powers of the county were arrayed against him, and he called the roll—the judge, the sheriff, the school superintendent, the tax assessor, and the county clerk. But Fess was not alone. "The people are on my side, and the people and I will win this fight together!"

The judge dashed home and put on a clean dry suit, then returned to the fray. A warrant was issued charging Fess Whitaker with assault and battery—with "willfully and knowingly propelling a quantity of buttermilk upon and against the body, person, arms, and limbs of the affiant, Sam Collins," and the "high sheriff" was commanded to arrest the miscreant forthwith. But when the sheriff appeared he found the gates barred, the steel door securely locked, and Fess safely within. The sheriff could not arrest the jailer but Fess could and did harangue the crowds.

128

Fess won by a tremendous margin. The state's largest newspaper hailed his victory with the headline: "Jailed Jailer elected Judge of Letcher County."

But still there was that warrant, and Sam Collins would be the judge for fifty-eight more days. Fess dared not venture forth from his iron and stone redoubt. Then the governor of Kentucky came to his rescue and issued a pardon that made Fess free and safe again. It bore the great seal and granted corporal safety and immunity from all charges and complaints whatsoever to the date thereof.

Fess emerged from the jail with a huge pitcher of buttermilk in his hands. He told the enraptured multitude that he was looking for Sam Collins to baptize him again, but Collins had fled. For years Collins was known as "Buttermilk Sam." The victorious Fess had crushed all his foes.

Fess's brother Gideon or "Gid" was a dentist at Whitesburg for a half century. He and Jim came to consult me about a stand of timber they proposed to buy and remained to tell me about Fess's memorable return to the jailer's office in 1925 and 1929.

In those days most blacks deemed themselves to be totally outside the political system. Their schools were trifling or nonexistent. Law enforcement scarcely extended to their end of the coal camp. Nearly all were Republicans but the GOP paid them no heed. Their memories of Deep South politics caused them to dislike the Democrats, a situation that changed dramatically with the coming of the New Deal. In Fess's time and region nearly all blacks voted because they were paid to do so. If they were not paid they sullenly stayed home.

In 1925 Judge Fess Whitaker's effort to switch back to the jailer's office was strongly opposed by the GOP's formal organization. To a man the county's old guard were determined to rid the party of this upstart Democrat-turned-Republican. The organization had plenty of money and, unfortunately but predictably, Fess had spent all of his. The "organization" would overwhelm him in the coalfield "black belt." Isolated families of blacks lived in several communities, but at least 95 percent of them were concentrated in the mining towns of Haymond, Fleming, McRoberts, Jenkins, and the dismal dens of Acme Hill overlooking the trifling town of Neon.

But Fess was not without resources of his own. The "slate" scheduled a barbecue with plenty of beer, and the blacks turned out by the hundreds to hear the speeches and find out what the pay-off would be. Fess's opponent and other invited candidates inveighed mightily against the incumbent judge and his iniquitous attempt to return to the jailer's office. He was, they said, a turncoat Democrat and an enemy of black people. They conjured up the ghost of Abraham Lincoln, the glorious emancipator, and urged that Fess Whitaker be sent back to join the "other Democrats who tried so hard to keep the honest black people in poverty and chains."

These remarks made a deep impression on the blacks and they glowered at the impudent Fess who had come unbidden to circulate in the crowd and consume some of the beer, bread, and beef. When the "program of speeches" ended, Fess strode to the platform and demanded a chance to speak also. The thunderstruck presiding officer acquiesced and Fess took the floor.

He waxed eloquent. He told them about Santiago and San Juan Hill, and Teddy Roosevelt. There were, he asserted, two "lines of Whitakers" in the county, the "red set" and the "black set." The red Whitakers were Democrats and part Indian while the black set were Republicans and part Negro. His good old mother was "like this wonderful lady here on the front row," he said, pointing, and rushed down from the platform to embrace her. With tears flowing down his cheeks he promised five dollars a vote instead of the two dollars mentioned by his opponent. He would be generous, he swore, generous and straight with the "great colored race."

On election day Fess appeared at the precincts and paid a full five dollars to each voter. He did it by check, too, drawn on the First National Bank at Whitesburg, with each one reading "For One Vote." He got their votes but, alas, when the checks were tendered for payment there was no money. As for Fess, on the day following the election he vanished on a glorious spree to celebrate his victory.

Fess's enemies, both black and white, waited with impatience for 1929 and a settling of old scores. But Fess gave the beer and barbecue party this time, advertising it for election eve. Again there was a spitted ox turning over a glowing pit, boxes of bread, and kegs of beer. A local band called the Ink Spots produced jivey music. Fess spoke to the assembled host and their wrath over the betrayal of four years ago evaporated.

Fess again alluded to San Juan Hill and the wall behind which he and Teddy sheltered. The story took a strikingly different turn this time, though. The Americans were pinned down by the fire from those devilish Mausers, dying by hundreds on every hand. He and Teddy bade one another farewell with parting handshakes. Then, there appeared a cloud of dust on the distant horizon—a cloud that turned into a regiment of Negro cavalry. Those fearless horsemen rescued the Rough Riders at the last desperate moment, slashed off Spanish heads with their sabers, and put the proud dons to flight.

Fess wept unrestrainedly as he recalled his brave black comrades.

Then he explained those cold checks. It was all the fault of his political enemies who had treacherously filed a groundless lawsuit and tied up his funds. Now the suit was settled. Fess had won, and his money was available in the bank. Every one of the old checks would be paid off on the day after the election. If anyone had lost his check in the intervening years a new one would be issued to replace it. And for tomorrow's election Fess was paying "five dollars straight"—by check.

The voters were reconciled to their old friend. They lined up and Fess wrote checks at a furious rate. There were hundreds of them—some for old votes and some for new. He hugged the ladies, fondling somewhat lasciviously the young and shapely ones, and carried the precincts in a landslide.

But when the checks were presented for payment there was

131

still no money. The hoax had worked even more effectively than it had the first time. And, as before, he was "out of town" on a mighty victory celebration!

Fess made one more race. He decided that an old war buddy of Theodore Roosevelt should sit with the mighty in Congress. The district's representative, "Big John" Langley, had been sent to the penitentiary for a violation of the Volstead Act and the whiskey-prone populace had promptly elected his wife Katherine to serve as a seat warmer until Big John's release. She had ample funding and the wholehearted support of the district's entrenched Republican power. She benefited from the sympathy generated by the "crucifixion" of her husband. Fess, on the other hand, had only his tongue and boundless energy.

Somehow he obtained a photograph of the good woman in the dreadful beachwear of the day. She wore a hideous and immense floppy hat and many folds of concealing garments. Then, too, it must be admitted that she was not beautiful. Fess had the picture blown up to lifesize and pasted on a specially made wooden frame. He took it with him on his speaking tours. He covered the thing in a mysterious cloth and carried it onto the speaker's platform. He would ridicule her for a while, then "introduce" his opponent. Off would come the cloth and the crowd would go wild with glee at the sight of the grinning figure in that monstrous costume.

Fess declared that he was a "straight shooter" and would tell only the truth. He illustrated by explaining that when he was in the army he was the finest marksman in the Coast Artillery. His target was a floating platform twelve feet square with a canvas superstructure that bore a black stripe six inches wide for improved visibility. The target was twenty-two miles out at sea and was pulled by a tugboat going sixteen knots. Fess fired fourteen-inch shells that weighed 2,250 pounds and used 640 pounds of powder. He loaded and fired at 16-second intervals. Out of five shots, four hit the target. One hit the black stripe dead center.

"That," Fess assured them, "is the kind of man the good

132

people of these hills ought to send to the United States Congress!"

Fess almost won. In his only race beyond the borders of his own county, against the opposition of the abundantly financed courthouse cliques everywhere, with virtually no funds of his own, and with only the humble office of county jailer as a springboard, he fell short of his goal by a mere 480 votes in a district composed of nine counties with a combined population of 420,000.

Fess was generally regarded as unbeatable in a new race for Congress. He had become well known in all the counties and his big grin, enormous hand, and unfailing spiel were eagerly awaited. But his career was cut short. On a summer day he imbibed too much of his beloved moonshine. He and a comely lady friend were whooping it up in his new Model A Ford when Fess lost control. His lady friend emerged from the wreck with a broken nose. Fess had a broken neck.

Fess was an Appalachian Huey Long. With a little additional luck and a bit more time the boy who never spoke a word until he was nine years old might have made it to the United States Senate. He had the three metallic qualities Abraham Lincoln said were necessary for political success—iron in his heart, brass in his face, and silver in his tongue.

A Juvenile Offender
Is Reformed

THE MAN who told me this story about himself is my friend and confidant and for many years was my client. I will not use his true name but will refer to him as Eb Holly.

I met him first in 1946, a newly demobilized sergeant from Patton's army. He had served with distinction under the "Old Man," and with much pride displayed his medals and a citation signed by "Old Blood and Guts" himself.

A year or two later he married. He and his wife were devoted to one another, and eventually there were three daughters. With a miner's wages he bought some land and built a neat frame house on it. As the family grew, so did the house, taking on a couple of two-room additions. In a neighborhood that was littered and junk-strewn, his home stood out as a model of neatness and order. The sergeant in him required that, and besides, his wife was a scrupulous housekeeper. The lawn was green and the carefully tended garden gleamed with a dozen varieties of vegetables.

The girls grew to levelheaded womanhood. All were educated, one as a teacher and the others as registered nurses. Eb was a PTA regular and active in efforts to improve the schools, establish a public library, and finance a public health clinic. He had considerable local influence in the Democratic party, sometimes serving as precinct chairman. He was a frequent donor at the county blood bank. His local of the United Mine Workers twice elected him president. He was the kind of solid citizen whose efforts and example make democracy function.

His life was not always so unblemished, however. There was a time when he stood humble and fearful before a judge, a convicted law violator awaiting sentence. That was the moment he described to me forty years after the event when he was a respectable and established fifty-six.

During Prohibition there was much coal mining in the Kentucky hills, but a solid majority of the people still lived on subsistence farms strung out along hundreds of winding creeks and their branches. These farms were nearly vertical affairs, extending from the narrow bottom lands up the steepening slopes almost to the broken cap-rocks. Agriculture was extremely primitive, relying on freshly cleared "new ground" to supply fertile soil for the bull-tongue plows. The trouble was that practically all the land had been cleared, and few primal coves remained. The people knew nothing about soil regeneration through cover crops, and pelting rains washed the loam away soon after the protective trees were cut down. Consequently, the farm people were locked into a descending spiral. The land produced less and less corn, which meant fewer chickens and hogs and less milk each year. Babies continued to come with annual regularity and the pinch tightened. All who could do so found work in the mines, but the rest had to seek livelihood elsewhere. Thousands left the region in a mammoth migration to Ohio and Michigan. Of those who remained, a substantial number were more or less saved by Prohibition.

Since time immemorial southern mountaineers had known how to make whiskey. Substantial numbers were of Irish and Ulster stock, and their forebears had brought the craft with them from the misty coves of their homeland. Others were descendants of Highland Scots to whom "wee nips" were deemed indispensable to physical and spiritual health. When they commingled with English settlers in the backwoods, the latter learned fast, and soon practically every cabin had its pot still smoking at

135

a nearby stream. In early times whiskey was the universal remedy, prescribed for snakebite, weak appetites, toothaches, insomnia, and chills and fevers.

As the nation grew, its thirst provided a market for backwoods industry. The fields yielded grain for the mash barrels, and the corn went to market as a distilled liquid. The hill people learned to make white oak barrels bound with strips of hickory bark in lieu of metal hoops. This crude cooperage was charred on the inside, filled with the raw new whiskey, and sealed for aging. At this point the barrels were loaded onto rafts and floated down the rivers for sale in the "spirits markets" in the settlements at Frankfort and along the Ohio. The buyers executed bond to assure payment of federal taxes, and in time this "bonded" whiskey became gentle enough to be advertised as "mild and mellow." The mountaineers went home with enough cash to tide them over to the next year, and the public's thirst was slaked.

Other mountaineers retailed whiskey from their own stills. The Treasury Department appointed local "storekeeper gaugers" to test the product for quality and "proof," and to collect the taxes due Uncle Sam. All these distilling and sales activities were entirely legal and constituted what we would now call a "cottage industry."

Gradually things changed. The government had trouble collecting its levies from numerous widely scattered stills. Some operators hid their works and sold their product untaxed. Losses to the Treasury mounted, and big corporate-owned distillers complained that they were being undersold by "fly-by-night" and "moonshine" competitors. Gradually Congress legislated a cordon of restrictions around the family stills. The required paperwork swamped the stiller who tried to stay within the law. At last the law was amended to require payment of the taxes by the producer when the whiskey went into the barrel for aging, or execution of a costly surety bond as a guarantee. These were beyond the small producer's capacity, and the "legal stiller" vanished. Thereafter he had to earn his money by other means or follow his ancestral calling as an outlaw. The latter course was tempting because he still had the knowledge and means for producing the fluid, and the market for it was not diminished by the federal revenue laws. When Prohibition came, the market boomed. In fact, the demand became insatiable at precisely the same time when land exhaustion was compelling the people to abandon farming. The solution to their problem was apparent: grow relatively small patches of corn, sell it as whiskey, and use the money to buy the meal, flour, meat, and clothing earlier generations had derived from the soil.

In the Cumberlands, circumstances combined to make the distilling and distribution of whiskey more profitable than ever before. The boom roared along throughout the 1920s. The moonshiners turned the stuff out at thousands of hidden stills in remote coves, in worked-out coal mines, and in natural caves. Bootleggers conveyed it to eager multitudes who "voted dry and drank wet."

Eb Holly's family lived on Pine Creek, which joins the North Fork of the Kentucky River seven miles below its source springs. Even after Pine Creek adds its piddling contribution, the Kentucky is no wider than a suburban living room. The confluence is at a tiny hamlet called Mayking. Eb's ancestors had lived there since 1800.

When the spring of 1930 came, Eb's father had a forty-gallon still operating in a deep, thickety hollow high on the steep north slope of the Pine Mountain. Above it loomed the gray shadow of the "Box Rock," an immense, towering outcrop of the mountain's sandstone rim. To prevent the formation of telltale paths, the still was visited as infrequently as its proper maintenance would permit and then by differing and circuitous approaches. Fires were kept to a minimum. When a "run" was under way the work proceeded at a feverish pace to lessen the likelihood of discovery.

Eb's uncles had similar stills in similar hollows. So did his cousins and their cousins. So, also, did one of his grandfathers. Even though the stills were their livelihood, the prospering owners of these operations seldom went about them or did any of the whiskey making. These tasks—and the risks of detection—were left to the children.

Cunning "revenuers" had made life a perpetual hell for the stillers. Hundreds of mountaineers had been hauled off to Atlanta and Leavenworth. They invariably returned in better shape than when they left, their rotten teeth extracted or mended, their frames filled out with regular and ample meals. Still, the sojourns were unpopular. Every conceivable device was resorted to in the battle of wits with the revenuers. One of these tactics involved the use of well-coached children. They were taught the work at an early age, and then made into full-time stillers.

If all went well, Pap got the money. If things went wrong, the children swore through thick and thin that Pap didn't know about it. The child was drilled as thoroughly as a ten-year private, sticking to the memorized refrain through interrogation by raiders, federal attorneys, and even judges. "Pap didn't know a thing about it. I never told Pap what I was a-doin'. He never knowed." If the juvenile stillers held fast, that was the end of the matter so far as the adults were concerned, because they invariably insisted that they had been otherwise engaged and had supposed the children were fishing or hunting or out on the hills digging ginseng and yellow root. The ploy worked so well that eventually nearly a third of the juvenile offenders charged in the entire federal court system were in the eastern district of Kentucky.

Thus it was that Eb Holly tended the family still on an April morning in that memorable year of the Great Depression. He was alone at the time, almost man-size at fifteen, and thoroughly skilled in his intricate work. His proud father had termed him a "natural-born stiller." The run was proceeding without a hitch, the clear sparkling fluid trickling steadily. He felt good and self-confident, pleased to be trusted with so important a function. They had outwitted the law for a long time, and it seemed they would be equally successful with this batch. Soon the jars would be filled, the whiskey ready to "cut" with pure.

water from a limestone spring. The slop would be disposed of, the barrels washed out and made ready for a fresh batch.

Eb's father had an arrangement with a crew on the Louisville and Nashville Railroad. Once or twice a week their train brought carloads of groceries from Cincinnati to wholesale firms and company commissaries. Most of the cars were empty on the return trip to the yards at DeCoursey in northern Kentucky. The empty train had to wait on a siding for an hour to permit the passage of coal "drags." This took place near midnight a couple of miles upriver from Mayking. For a considerable share of the selling price, the trainmen allowed Eb's father to load his whiskey into an empty boxcar, from which it was carefully lifted by gentlemen from Cincinnati while the train idled in similar seclusion near the Ohio River some twenty-four hours later. Lonesome nocturnal whistle toots often had meaning only to moonshiners and bootleggers.

Eb reflected on all this as he worked. He thought of the new shoes and clothing he had been promised out of the "liquor money." He was mightily satisfied with himself and considered that, all things considered, this was a highly satisfactory way of making a living.

But this whiskey would never be sold. A voice spoke from behind Eb, a voice of authority and absolute finality, "Don't move a step, young man. Stay right where you are! Now, turn around with your hands up."

Eb's heart turned to lead as he obeyed. There a dozen steps away stood Clark Day, a pistol in his hand. Just behind him were two other men whom Eb had never seen. Like Day, they wore shiny badges on their jackets. Each of them gripped a Winchester rifle. Day was known far and wide for his ruthless "still cutting," and after he had slipped handcuffs onto Eb's wrists he took a hatchet from a scabbard at his waist and systematically destroyed the entire still, its copper coil or "worm," the barrels, and the fruit jars. When he had finished, the family's source of income was a worthless ruin.

This sudden turn of events put a new light on things, but Eb stuck to his guns. Any admission that his father and other relatives were involved would send them straight to the penitentiary and turn him into a despised outcast. He would be loathed as a "squealer" who had betrayed his own blood. Consequently his answers to the ensuing interrogation were short and undeviating.

The questioning had its brutal aspects. The "revenuers" knew him and his father and uncles. They knew he would lie to protect his elders and that he was lying from the first word of his first reply. They pleaded with him to tell the truth and promised him immunity from prosecution if he would do so. Then they turned nasty, cocked their guns, and threatened to "blow out his trashy, Goddamned brains" unless he changed his answers. But Eb stood firm by the story he and his father had agreed on.

"Whose still is this?"

"Mine."

"Where did you get it?"

"Found it hid under a brush pile at the head of Cram Creek."

"Where did you get these barrels and fruit jars?"

"Same place."

"Who helped you bring 'em here?"

"Nobody. Brought 'em here by myself."

"Who helped you make this liquor?"

"Nobody. I made it."

"Who showed you how to make whiskey?"

"Nobody. I learned how from a magazine."

"Where did you get the magazine?"

"Found it in the wastecan at the post office."

"What was the name of the magazine?"

"I don't know. The cover was off and gone when I found it in the wastecan."

"Where did you get the corn this whiskey was made from?"

"Stole it from Pap's cornfield."

"Did your dad know you were here at this still?"

"No. I told him I was goin' to hunt groundhogs."

"Did you ever catch any groundhogs?"

"Plenty."

And so it went. Eb was marched off to the United States Commissioner at Whitesburg and released on a $2,000 appearance bond executed by his father and a couple of "accommodation cosigners." His father employed attorney Dave Hays to defend him on the indictment a federal grand jury was certain to return, and Eb went home to ponder the wages of sin.

Hays had emphasized that there was no escaping the charge itself. The facts precluded that. He would have to plead guilty and cast himself on "the mercy of the court." Judge A. M. J. Cochran was a stern man whose court was inundated by juvenile offenders, pregnant women bootleggers, and others whom, for practical reasons, it was virtually impossible to try or punish. Hays said, "If you do as I advise, and if the judge gets up feeling good on the day of your trial, you won't have to serve a day!"

Eb had rarely been to Whitesburg, a dusty village of 1,400, its streets still mostly dirt and cinders. He had never been outside the county at all, and the prospect of going to Pikeville and standing up in a courtroom filled with strangers to answer to a judge was appalling. The indictment would be handed down at a special term in August and court would reconvene in October. For months he was preoccupied with the horror that had fallen on him. He lived in a nightmare of tension and dread that was only slowly relieved by unremitting parental reassurances.

Morning, noon, and night his father and mother told him not to worry, that everything would turn out all right. He was only fifteen, too young to be sent to the penitentiary. He could be sent to a center for juvenile offenders, but the judge would not do that because his was a first offense. And besides, the juvenile centers were all jam-packed with "drifters," boys and girls who wandered the countryside as economic orphans of the coalfield depression. Whether he wanted to or not, the "old judge" would have to order probation in the custody of his parents. He had no other choice to speak of. Besides, Dave Hays was a fine criminal lawyer and he said Cochran's hands were tied by circumstances beyond his control. "Just do as the lawyer tells you

141

and everything will turn out fine," his father allowed. His mother brought her voice to support the same pleasant prospect and added, "You wouldn't have got ketched in the first place if you hadn't made that run on Sunday. The Lord won't let a body profit from Sunday work." Gradually his courage and self-confidence returned, and when his trial day came he was almost cocky.

Hays had a room at the Hatcher Hotel and arranged for his youthful client to spend the night with him. When court was called to order the next morning Eb was decked out in a white shirt with an uncomfortable tie about his neck. He had on a suit his father had acquired at East Jenkins and looked more like an overgrown country bumpkin on his way to college than a moonshiner headed for the dock. That, of course, was precisely the impression his lawyer wanted to convey.

Court opened with a bewildering array of guilty-looking defendants, nearly all charged with Prohibition violations. One after another they came before the judge for arraignment. Some entered pleas of not guilty and had their trials assigned for "days certain" at which they were admonished to be "present and ready." Most said they were guilty. Some of these were sentenced then and there, as repeat offenders. Many of the others were questioned and lectured. After all, the judge's hands *were* tied. The prisons and juvenile centers *were* full—a decade of unmatched criminality had seen to that. A vexed and weary judge was largely helpless before a veritable avalanche of simple, ill-clothed country women and slouching, unkempt boys and girls. He could hope they would mend their ways, but he knew too much about human nature to expect it. With the prisoners who came so interminably to stand before him the judge was locked in a futile charade that ground on and on, seemingly without end or purpose.

At last the clerk cried, "The United States of America versus Eb Holly." Eb's heart leaped, almost stopping entirely. His lawyer rose, motioned him to follow, and stood before the bar in front of the bench. Through the pounding of blood in his ears he

142

heard as if from a great distance Hays's voice as he told the court the plea was "guilty." Judge and lawyer discussed his case and the latter said there were "extenuating circumstances." The Court listened dubiously and said he would consider such circumstances. "The defendant has a statement he would like to make, Your Honor," the lawyer intoned. Judge Cochran leaned back in his high swivel chair. "Of course, I will hear anything he has to say to me," he declared.

Suddenly Eb had the floor. Every eye was on him, every ear strained to catch what he would say. The lined Scotch-Irish face of the judge, snowy sideburns on his cheeks, loomed above him. Eb looked at the judge, compelled himself not to look away, and with as much conviction as he could muster recited the sentences he had been practicing for six months.

"Judge, Your Honor," he said, with a voice that strove to sound sincere and respectful, "I know I have made a terrible mistake and I regret it. I violated the law and there can't be any good excuse for that. I can't undo what I have already done, but I can straighten out and be a good citizen from here on out."

Judge Cochran watched him intently as he went on. "I realize that I am off on the wrong foot in life, and on a road that leads nowhere. If you decide to spare me from prison, I have made up my mind to go back to school, finish high school, and go to Berea College. I may study to become a school teacher. Anyway, there will be no more moonshinin', you can count on that!"

Eb glanced at Dave Hays. The lawyer seemed pleased with the sound of his own words emerging from his client's lips. Not too servile, Hays thought, and no trace of insincerity or arrogance. Humbleness and straightforwardness, the kind of pitch that generally works.

Eb concluded with a plea for another chance. "The world is full of people who have done wrong and then gone straight for the rest of their lives. That's what I want to do." He looked at his lawyer to signal the end of his plea. Hays indicated that he had nothing to add.

Judge Cochran leaned forward, hawklike eyes boring into Eb's. A huge, age-withered hand clutched his gavel. "Young man," he rumbled in a low voice that carried to every part of the courtroom, "you have had fifteen years to think about what you have just said to me. You have had fifteen years to consider right and wrong and to choose between them, and you chose to violate the law—to do wrong. You may mean what you have told me and you may not. Only you know what is in your heart. But flagrant violations cannot go unpunished, especially in husky, young fellows like yourself. Accordingly, you are sentenced to serve six months at hard labor in a federal center for juvenile offenders. When you get out, we'll see how you behave and whether you become a good citizen or a persistent criminal."

A marshall abruptly led the crestfallen youth to a cell, and the next day he was delivered to the warden of the juvenile center designated in the court's order. He spent five months working on the prison farm, as well as in the laundry, kitchen, and bakery, and attending eighth-grade level classes. The work was hard. The rules were strict and the discipline was tight. The premises were crowded and there was scarcely a pleasant moment in the entire interlude. His term shortened for good behavior, he was sent home wearing the new suit his father had bought him for the trial and with twenty-five dollars in cash.

When he ended his story, I commiserated with him, commenting that the judge's decision seemed harsh in view of Eb's youth at the time and his extraordinary pledge of good behavior for the future. But Eb would not have it. He disagreed sharply. "Judge Cochran was absolutely right," he asserted. "I had not reformed. I was lying to him. If he had probated me, I would have been back at a still in less than a month and would have gone from bad to worse. He made a believer out of me, and a man, too!"

Bad John Wright

JOHN WRIGHT died at the age of eighty-eight. In that long span he lived a varied life and accomplished most of the things he undertook. He was called "Bad John" because he was not one to be tampered with. Tradition puts the number of men he killed at twenty-two but he said the figure was exaggerated. He admitted that there were seven at least. He claimed he killed no one who did not richly deserve it, and if he had slain all of his contemporaries who merited that fate he would have been an exceedingly active man. It is doubtful that any of the men who fell to his "Navy .44" took with them much of the world's sweetness and light.

John was a man of many parts: soldier, circus performer, deputy United States marshal, deputy sheriff, manhunter, and woman-catcher. From beginning to end he was fond of womanly flesh.

I grew up on tales about him. According to my grandmother he was a member of my grandfather's cavalry platoon when that ill-fated unit was captured by Union soldiers at Gladeville, Virginia. "A right smart little battle" preceded the surrender. The rebels were in the brick courthouse when they waved a white rag tied to the end of a ramrod. John was the youngest rebel in the lot, a handsome nineteen. The Confederates came out with their hands high, their little fortress ringed by bayonets. A Yankee captain advanced to meet them, his fingers grasping the reins of a splendid black horse. Private Wright was at the rear of the vanquished Confederates. Suddenly he jerked a concealed pistol out of his shirt and rushed forward, shot the unfortunate captain in the face, and leaped onto his saddle. Bending low, he spurred the horse and dashed away amid a hail of misdirected bullets.

The perfidious murder of their captain aroused the wrath of the Union soldiers and they came "within a hair" of killing my grandfather and the rest of the rebels then and there. The intervention of a Northern lieutenant and their own fervent pleading saved their lives, but the Yankees applied their boots to their captives in a manner not countenanced by the rules of war.

Tilden Wright was Bad John's great-nephew, and died at ninety-two in 1975. Tilden was my client for many years and told me numerous stories about his uncle, most of which I heard also from others who traced their ancestry back to "grandpap Wright." Since John kept numerous ladies in his harem his descendants are legion.

According to Tilden, John went north after he escaped at Gladeville. He hid his butternut uniform in his saddlebags and put on civilian clothes he found in a house whose lawful owners had gone to church. In these garments he made his way to Ohio where prosperous farmers were paying $300 a head for substitutes to serve in the place of their sons in Lincoln's embattled legions. John picked up fifteen twenty-dollar gold pieces in this fashion, took the oath of a Union soldier, and put on a blue uniform. A couple of days later he deserted, donned the clothes he had acquired from the church-going Virginians, and received a federal bounty for reenlisting under another name. Two desertions and two enlistments later he was back in Kentucky with twelve hundred dollars in cash. He reached General John Hunt Morgan's command in time to help his old colors at the battle of Cynthiana in June 1864.

In that engagement a rifle ball struck John in the hip so that he walked with a limp for the rest of his life. The retreating rebels left him at a farmhouse where he was looked after by an apple-cheeked girl named Mattie Humphrey. John claimed her as his wife and eventually took her to his log cabin in Letcher County. One of his myriad granddaughters told me that John was true to her after a fashion—"She was always his favorite woman!"

As a "peace officer" John hunted numerous malefactors for the rewards offered for their capture dead or alive. If the way was long, he often brought them back dead as a matter of convenience. In 1884 John went to his friend J. Proctor Knott, governor of Kentucky, and showed him a warrant from a Letcher County justice of the peace for Claib Jones, "a notorious outlaw from Knott County." At John's request the governor proclaimed a reward of five hundred dollars for Claib's capture. A day or two later Jones arrived in Frankfort and laid before the governor a Knott County warrant charging Wright with numerous felonies. Governor Knott cheerfully set a five hundred dollar reward on Bad John's scalp also, and the two cutthroats hunted one another for years in an officially financed game of "may the best man win!"

John's friendship with Kentucky's Democratic governors—all veterans of the Confederate army—helped him immensely when the Republican officials of Pike County undertook to "persecute" him. John had grown fond of an unmarried woman who lived on remote Beef Hide Creek. John believed her house was in Letcher County and was outraged when the Pike County judge issued a warrant charging him with adultery. The Pike Countians maintained that the cabin where John had visited the lady was tucked just inside their county. This development presented a major dilemma: until the county lines were established, each visit to his love nest carried the possibility of arrest and imprisonment. So John went back to Frankfort to see the governor, who appointed a commission to "view out" the true and correct boundary line separating the two counties, and to fix it by "metes and bounds." The three commissioners worked with diligence and care, and determined that the line ran well to the east of the woman's modest cottage, a decision that placed the house safely within Letcher County. Henceforth, John need have no fear of posses directed by Union veterans entrenched in the courthouse at Pikeville.

Zack Bentley was police judge of the town of Neon for twelve years. He was a dignified old gentleman but in his youth his behavior left much to be desired. He once told me of an unfortunate brush he had with Bad John in 1898. John was fifty-three at the time and he taught the twenty-year-old Zachary Bentley some lessons he would never forget.

A klavern of the Ku Klux Klan had been organized in Letcher County and the Dragon was preaching a holy war against "lewdness." This moral defect, the Dragon intoned from behind his white duncecap and flowing robe, threatened to undermine the country. Lewdness would pervert the purity of Anglo-Saxon womanhood and result in females who would interbreed with Negroes. This would, without doubt, produce mulattoes, and the mongrelization of the master race would advance quickly. Before long the vitiated stock would be too weak to defend the rich continent God had bequeathed to Americans, and European and Asian kings would take over. As Uncle Zack recalled it, "He got people worked up to the point where all they could think of was the approaching end of the white race." There were no more than a score of blacks in the county, all of whom were much too humble to think of "debasing" a white woman. With no blacks to straighten out, the Dragon directed the knights to root out lewdness in ungodly white women. Before long, hapless ladies of easy virtue were feeling the Avenging Rod of Southern Manhood. "At the stroke of midnight" the victim would be awakened by the trampling of hooves and would peer out to see a circle of horsemen about her house, each figure clad in "the robes of terror," and carrying a blazing brand. "Summoned to judgment," she would hear her fate solemnly intoned and receive the prescribed number of lashes "well laid on."

There were not many lewd women, so the floggings were enlarged to include a few errant men. The county was terrified as the sore backs multiplied. Almost nightly, light sleepers caught glimpses of ghostly mounted figures on their nocturnal forays in defense of female chastity and racial purity.

148

Uncle Zack confessed, "Looking back on it, I can see now that we were a bunch of lunatics and every one of us ought to have been ambushed and shot. We had got ourselves to believing the biggest bunch of foolishness anybody ever heard of."

An ambush is precisely what Bad John had in mind. Some of the lewd women in question were, quite literally speaking, his bosom friends and he prepared a drastic counterstroke.

One night twenty sheeted forms rode past the mouth of Boone Creek on their way to a chastisement. Hidden in the brush by the roadside were Bad John and seven or eight of his henchmen. When the solemn procession was out of sight the "bushwhackers" went to work. They dismantled a nearby rail fence and brought the long slender timbers to a straight stretch of the narrow county road. On either side they raised a fence six feet high and reinforced it with stakes to assure its sturdiness. The parallel fences were about twelve feet apart and extended for fifty yards. At the end a barrier of the same staunch material completely obstructed the road. Thus the returning horsemen would ride into a narrow chute, a cul-de-sac. The trap was constructed where the road ran through a grove of elms whose branches spread deep, gloomy shadows over the structure. When the work was finished, John and his men took up positions behind trees and rocks near the open end of the trap. A weeping woman was about to be avenged.

Each man in John's party carried a huge pistol. Some carried Winchester rifles as additional artillery and others had double-barreled 12-gauge shotguns. As for John, his main weapon was a magazine-loading pump shotgun charged with .00 buck pellets—probably the most lethal hand-carried firearm available at that time.

(There was one exception to these heavy armaments: Wash Bates told me that John allowed him to go along "for the experience." He was nearly fifteen at the time and had no death-dealer other than a trifling nickel-plated .32 caliber revolver. He said, "I did my best with what I had.")

149

About 2 A.M. the nightriders returned. The moon was down, and in the elm grove the darkness was almost total. The hooves plopped solemnly in the sandy soil of the primitive road. As the last sheeted form passed the open end of the chute, John's men moved out into the road and knelt. All aimed straight down the fenced tunnel and waited.

Presently, a plodding horse plowed into the barricade and came to a halt. The majestic silence of the retinue was broken by an astonished oath. Other horses struck the foremost ones amid grunts, queries, and more oaths. At that moment John's shotgun went off, followed by a fiery and sustained fusillade. Every gun was firing toward the puzzled pileup at the end of the cul-de-sac. The shotguns and Winchesters boomed, the big pistols cracked, and the little revolver popped. The carnage was awesome.

Two knights leaped from their rearing mounts and escaped over the top of the fence. Others were shot down or crushed by the rearing and kicking horses. Zack and several others turned and charged the blazing guns. Their race for life occurred in that brief moment when John's men were shifting from emptied rifles and shotguns to loaded pistols, and several escaped. Zack said that as he dashed past the line of ambushers a pistol went off and in the muzzle-flash he saw "Tilden Wright's nose as plain as day."

That was the last of the Noble Knights. The Dragon and three others were dead amid a mound of torn sheets and dead horses. The wounded and captured were in "close custody." Zack and those who had followed his wild dash were lying low and planning vengeance. Zack said with a twinkle, "I never wanted to get even with anybody so bad in my life."

A week or so later these wrathful survivors met in an abandoned cabin to plot the end of John Wright. It was decided that joint action was too risky—a single killer must do the job. Straws were collected and trimmed to varying lengths, and each man selected one. Zack's straw was the shortest. To him would go the duty and distinction of killing "Bad John."

Zack's old comrades were to be arraigned on a Monday morning for their night riding activities, and John would certainly be present in the courtroom for the occasion. His current ladylove was a slim thirty-year-old who lived with her children in a cabin on Rock House Creek while she awaited the return of her husband from the state penitentiary. Zack calculated that John would leave his home at Payne Gap on Sunday afternoon and ride to this lady's abode. After a comforting night with her he would leave early to travel the remaining miles to the county seat. This course would take him through a low gap in the ridge at the head of Millstone Creek. There Zack would "get set."

When the soft light of dawn appeared, Zack was ready. He had taken up a position on a bed of moss behind a tree, his position concealed by wild ferns and low bushes. He was armed with a new .32-.20 lever action Winchester rifle. "Old John would ride right up from behind me," Zack explained, "then on through the gap and down Millstone Creek. When he did that I intended to shoot him in the back of the head."

The concealed rifleman waited. The ring of horseshoes reached him, and he sighted down the trail in anticipation, but the rider was a widow with a "turn of corn" in front of her sidesaddle. She was headed for a gristmill on the river. The cocked hammer was lowered, and the wait resumed.

Again the ring of steel on stone warned of the approach of a horse, and the hammer was drawn back. But Zack was disappointed a second time. A Methodist preacher was on his way to Whitesburg. Zack would see him later in the day loafing about the courthouse. A couple of others passed, but John did not come. Still Zack did not despair. His plan was sound and he would wait. John may have found an early morning diversion that accounted for his delay.

Suddenly a cold, implacable voice spoke a few yards behind Zack. "Drop that Winchester and turn over so I can see your face." Zack froze as if ice had run through his veins. His nerveless fingers released the rifle and he rolled over to look behind

151

him. There stood "Bad John," an immense .44 revolver in his hand aimed squarely at Zack, the hammer back at full cock. Zack wilted. John's lip curled in scorn. "So you thought you could outwit the old gray fox," he sneered. "I've killed more trash like you than I can remember right off!"

He had Zack pick up the Winchester by the end of the barrel and hand it to him. Then he marched Zack to the road. He took a rawhide string from his pocket and bound the youth's hands securely behind his back. This done, he went for his horse which he had tied to a sapling a couple of hundred yards away. On his return he gave Zack his instructions. "Bentley," he said, "it is ten miles to Whitesburg and I must be there in exactly one hour and fifty minutes. I intend to make the trip on time and be present when court opens. You will be there too. If you keep up with me and my horse you will be alive when we get there. If you don't keep up I'll shoot you and lay your carcass across my horse." His pale blue eyes were icy. "It's up to you."

Zack recalled the trip vividly. "I kept up," he grinned. "I reached the courthouse about five feet ahead of the horse. I didn't have any skin left on my feet, but I got there first. I knew good and well that Bad John never told anybody the same thing twice and I took him at his word."

At the county seat the sore-footed Zack was charged and led before the circuit judge with a half dozen other crestfallen knights of the Ku Klux Klan. All said they were not guilty and demanded jury trials.

They languished behind bars for three months until the next term of court, and changed circumstances saved them. The county was electrified by news of the outbreak of war with Spain, and patriotic fever swept the land. The fallen knights pleaded with Judge William Pearl to let them join the army and fight for their threatened country. John thought it was a good idea and told the judge so. "They might get killed," he counseled His Honor, "and we can always try them after the war is over!" The judge sent them under guard to the enlistment office at Lexington, two hundred miles away. His parting observation to them was along these consoling lines. "If the Spaniards kill every one of you we can be comforted by the knowledge that the county will stand up well under the loss!"

Zack said he didn't have anything against the Spaniards and managed to desert just before they reached Lexington. The others arrived safely, and in my youth were the silver-haired veterans of Cuba, San Juan, and the "Philippine Pacification Campaign." A forgiving judge dismissed the indictments after they returned victorious from all those bloody fields. When Bad John died, several of them attended his funeral.

Bad John's captives did pretty well for themselves. Boaz Adkins became a dentist, and I owe my mouthful of sound teeth to the things he told me as a boy. He was a frequent guest at our Sunday dinner table and summed Bad John up succinctly. "He was mean as hell!"

John D. W. Collins became a zealous law enforcement officer. During the prohibition era he was a treasury agent. He became a lawyer and was my colleague at the Letcher County bar for fifteen years. He had a splendid sense of humor. "Tee, hee," he giggled in his office one afternoon, a glass of bourbon and water in his hand. "We made the mistake of whipping one of Bad John's lewd women and he damn near killed every one of us because of it. I jumped over the fence and tried to run but my robe got tangled up in some briars and he caught me. That robe had five buckshot holes in it."

Morgan Reynolds escaped and "hid out" for a while. He was elected sheriff in 1923. He tried to enforce the law in a lawless county and had sixteen deputies shot to death in a four-year term. Three federal officers died with them. The population of Letcher County at that time was about 33,000.

Wash Bates lived a long life and in his old age was a justice of the peace. Almost to the end, his right front trouser pocket sagged beneath the weight of a small .32 caliber revolver. "The worst thing that can happen to a man," he informed me by way of explanation, "is to need a pistol and not have it!" Tilden Wright said that the dead Dragon had been hit in the back of the head by a small bullet—"about like a .32."

Money was short in the hills and John had to pick up sums the best way he could. One day he received a heartwarming missive from a resident of New York City. According to the author of the letter an unfortunate wretch languishing in a Mexican prison, his name yet unknown to the writer, had written warmly of John Wright. This thoughtful prisoner had stashed away a vast amount of cash which he wanted John and the gentleman in New York to share. The money was in a safe deposit box and the key would be theirs if the two would supply him with a mere twenty-two hundred dollars—eleven hundred each. This money would be used by John's imprisoned friend to bribe the warden, who would then permit the prisoner to escape. Thus the two who contributed the bribe money would divide an immense sum of ill-gotten loot, John's friend would escape from his Mexican cell, and the warden would have spending money. The whole undertaking would be simple and easy and foolproof. The gentleman concluded his letter with the hope that John would bring or send the money at once.

John replied without delay. Yes, he thought he knew the name of the unfortunate in Durango. He was probably Mrs. Wright's long-missing brother. John had mortgaged his farm and had his share of the money in hand. He would bring it to New York and gladly deliver it to his friend who had taken the trouble to write the kind letter. There was one hitch: the gentleman must meet John and show his own half of the money. In this way John would be assured that his new friend was honest and sincere, and not just taking advantage of a farmer who had never been away from home in his life.

Back came an answer. John would be met at the railway station by the undersigned himself. The undersigned would produce his eleven hundred dollars, collect John's contribution, and be on his way. A few days later the undersigned would return from

Durango with the deposit box key, the two friends would open the box, and the treasure would be theirs in equal shares.

John got off a letter agreeing fully to the arrangement and stating the day and hour of his arrival. He put eleven hundred dollars in "greenbacks" in his coat pocket and a clean shirt and socks in his valise. He dropped a limber, well-weighted black-jack into the bag and took along his trusty .44 revolver in a shoulder holster.

He rode a horse to Stonega, Virginia, the nearest railhead. There he caught a train and in due time arrived at Pennsylvania Station. With his humble suitcase he looked the part of a country bumpkin making his first journey to Gotham.

He was not quite so innocent. He had spent a considerable stretch with P. T. Barnum's circus—"the Greatest Show on Earth"—in which he was billed as the finest marksman in the wild and woolly West. His pistol unerringly shattered fragile targets while he ran, rode, and stood on his head. Part of this was due to genuine skill and endless practice. The rest was attributable to the nature of his Colt .45 revolver. It was a huge smoothbore, and each cartridge was loaded with a charge of birdshot. He had visited most large American cities and three European capitals with this act. In him the con gang had chosen a strange victim upon whom to work the ancient Mexican prisoner fraud.

John stepped off the train and was hailed by an "Italian-looking" gentleman who shook hands as John expressed his heartfelt gratitude to his helpful new friend.

The Italian-looking gentleman bought John a fine lunch of oysters and delicate little potato cakes. He made many inquiries about "Mr. Wright," his family, and friends. He overflowed with optimism and good wishes. Then he looked at his watch. They must get down to business, and John suggested that they go to the men's room. There John would see the other's cash and deliver his own. The facilities were unoccupied at the moment, and John produced an envelope full of cash and displayed it to his benefactor. The other did likewise and John thumbed through it to make sure he was not being shortchanged. Then he pulled out the .44 and motioned toward one of the empty toilet stalls. "In there!" he commanded with a sharp poke in the ribs. The astonished con man followed orders, a ghastly expression on his swarthy face. "Sit down," John said, indicating the only seat. The blackjack crashed down on the round, balding skull, and John's fellow crook slumped "cold as kraut." The blackjack and both packets of money went into the valise, and the pistol was returned to the holster. A few moments later John mounted the steps of a southbound train. In the meantime the man who had paid for his lunch struggled to regain consciousness and to reconstruct the painful events that had brought him to his difficult situation.

John's reputation for straightforward dealings brought him into contact with many distinguished characters. He was always ready to help an old Confederate war veteran, and in this capacity, according to great-nephew Tilden, he was able to do "a real favor" for Jesse Woodson James.

As all good rebel sympathizers know, Jesse James was an upright country boy who was driven to crime by a combination of double-crossing Yankees to whom he had innocently surrendered, and crooked bankers who held mortgages on the homes of widows. In a sturdy attempt to straighten things out he and his gang robbed numerous banks that were foreclosing unjustly on the aforesaid widows. This caused the gang to flee from pillar to post, and one such foray brought them into hiding near Ironton, Ohio. There they lay hidden in a stock barn while the farmer brought them food and rumors. They kept the farmer's fourteen-year-old son as a hostage "just in case his old man got greedy for the rewards," and wore themselves out trying to think of some way to escape the army of sheriff's deputies, United States marshals, posses, Pinkerton detectives, reward hunters, and militiamen who were scouring the country for their blood.

At length Jesse suggested to the farmer that he travel southward into Kentucky and up the Big Sandy to the home of John W. Wright. He would deliver a sealed letter to Mr. Wright and await developments. In the meantime, the boy would remain in the barn while his mother provided food for her guests. If all went well the lad would be released safe and sound, and the farmer would be abundantly paid for his services in their behalf.

After a six-day journey the Ohioan finally slept in one of John's beds. The letter he had carried told John about Jesse's dilemma and the $44,000 the latter had accumulated. If John would bring a band of men to Ohio and provide the James gang safe passage across Kentucky into Tennessee, he would be helping men who had shared his suffering in the Lost Cause. On the Tennessee line they would split the loot fifty-fifty. Twenty-two thousand dollars was an immense sum in an age when a day laborer received fifty cents for ten hours of work.

John told the farmer to rest a few days. Messengers went out and an army began assembling. Three days after his arrival the uneasy Ohioan counted twenty-two mounted men at John's cabin. They were lean, mustached, stoop-shouldered, lanky, and willing to kill for slight cause. They were loaded down with firearms. Each man carried at least one pistol, though several had two. Each also had a Winchester or Sharp's rifle. Their saddlebags bulged with cartridges and "grub." They left before dawn the next morning, an army of John Wright's kinsmen and former comrades-in-arms.

John knew "nigh ways" and shortcuts through Magoffin, Morgan, and Elliott counties. The country was sparsely populated and feud-ridden, and people who observed their passage thought it best to see nothing. They were ferried to the Ohio shore after darkness fell, and reached the hideout near midnight. When the farmer delivered John's message, the nervous outlaws received John for a conference. Within minutes the farmer was $500 richer and the two gangs had vanished.

The combined bands were immune from attack or challenge and went southward over the same trails the Kentuckians had followed on their way north. At John's home there were food and beds; then the trek continued through Harlan and Bell counties to the Cumberland Gap. There John and Jesse conferred out of sight and hearing of the others and John's saddlebags took in the promised $22,000. When the two bands separated the men shook hands all around. Jesse and Frank said they liked the Kentucky hills and might come there to live someday. John thought a place could be found for them. "We might elect one of you sheriff," he jested.

Then the James gang were swallowed by the darkness and the Tennessee hills. Robert Ford rode just behind Jesse and to his left.

Tilden said the money was not all profit, though. John appreciated the help his men had given him on the expedition and paid each of them a hundred dollars. Ninety percent of the take was enough for the chief.

Many years after I first heard this unlikely story, Mattie Wright Houston came to see me about the small estate she expected to leave her children. She was frail and thin with age, and one of the last surviving grandchildren of "Bad John." When she rose to leave I asked her whether she had ever heard him speak of Jesse James.

"Yes, I did," she responded. "When grandpap and grandma were old I stayed with them a lot. I was young at the time and empty-headed like girls often are. Grandpap had a lot of guns and one day he undertook to clean and oil them. I didn't have anything else to do so I sat down and watched.

"Each time he would take up a gun to work on it I would ask, 'Grandpap, where did you get that gun?' and he would tell me. He had took most of them off men he killed. He said they were souvenirs."

Then she laughed because she had known Zack as long as she could remember. "Grandpap showed me a rifle-gun and said he took it off Zack Bentley. He said Zack was too big for his britches in his young days.

"Finally he come to a pistol with pretty pearl handles and I said, 'Grandpap, where did you get that one?' He picked it up and looked at it, and thought a little before he answered. 'Honey, Jesse James gave me that pistol. I did him a great favor once and he seemed to appreciate it a mighty lot. When I left him he said, *Here, Wright, this is for you—a gift from Jesse James!*'"

When Bad John was about sixty a bloody feud broke out between his kinfolks and their neighbors, the Reynoldses. He went on the assumption that blood is thicker than water, and helped out his nephews and their warring progeny. In one of his last gunfights he tangled with John Reynolds, a redoubtable soul who was armed with a .50 caliber "buffalo rifle." The immense bullets contained explosive caps that blew up on contact. John was drawing a bead on Reynolds with his .44 revolver when one of those potent bullets struck the tree behind which he sheltered. The resulting explosion knocked out an eye so that in his old age he was both lame and one-eyed.

John always helped his friends and thwarted his enemies whenever possible. Hiram Hall, an elderly mountaineer from Knott County, described John's effort to "help" his Uncle Talt when that felon lay in the jail at Wise, Virginia, awaiting the hangman's noose.

"Bad Talt" Hall was John's blood kin and had fought and slain for Wright on many occasions. When he was arrested and tried in Virginia, he was wanted for murder in two other jurisdictions as well—Kentucky and New Mexico Territory. In the latter he shot down three cowboys who undertook to punish him for refusing to buy drinks in his turn. After all, they had bought and he had drunk, and they were not about to tolerate his stinginess when called upon to treat. They went to the graveyard and Talt fled. He got to Wise County—only twenty miles from his home in Kentucky—where he impetuously killed a policeman. Bad Talt had come to the end of his days.

John went to visit him and they had a long talk. Talt sent "last words" to many people—greetings, farewells, and exhortations. The jail was built of thick-walled stone, fenced with high steel pikes, and fitted with massive doors. Neither John nor Talt could think of a means by which a raiding party from Kentucky could rescue him. John told him the truth, "Talt, you've got to go!"

Still when John went back to Kentucky, Talt made a boast. The jailer told the sheriff and the proud prediction flew far and wide. "They will never hang Talt Hall!"

The Virginia governor sent fifty militiamen to the little crossroads called Wise Courthouse, and they guarded the jail and scaffold night and day. Not even an army of Kentuckians could carry Talt away. On September 2, 1892, Talt walked from his cell to the gallows. He climbed the steps and his hands were bound behind his back. His ankles were secured and the noose was placed about his neck. Talt wore a clean white shirt for the occasion and his voice was strong and clear. He said he wanted to make a final statement. The sheriff consented and Talt talked for half an hour. He rambled about many subjects. He began calmly and with self-assurance, but his voice gradually changed and became husky. He dropped out of sight a broken and desolate man.

His nephew told me the cause of his distress. It was not fear of death, because Talt was a brave man. It was disappointment.

John had assured Talt he would never hang. A marksman would be stationed on a distant elevation and would aim at the center of Talt's white shirt as he stood on the gallows. At his uncle's bidding a Wright youth, then a soldier in the United States Army, had stolen a long Krag rifle from a barrack in Alabama. The rifle had tremendous range, firing a copper-jacketed bullet in a straight and true line for thousands of yards. Talt would die when one of those bullets flashed through his heart.

The hanging day was bright and clear, perfect for good shooting. When Talt climbed the scaffold he looked about, and there southward toward Kentucky at the agreed place he saw movement. Bad John had kept his word.

Hiram Hall said that all of John's efforts were thwarted by "just plain accident." Among those who attended the hanging was a farmer from some remote mountain hollow. He had arrived early and bought his wife a large mirror for her kitchen or bedroom. Then he hastened to the courtyard. The mirror was not wrapped, and he held it in his arms as he listened to the doomed man speak. He was just beneath Talt and slightly to one side, and could look up at his haggard face. As the rays of the ascending sun bored into the mirror, they were mightily magnified and flung back. The distant marksman peered down the sights of his superb rifle but could not see the white shirt, or Talt, or even the gallows. He saw only a blob of blinding sunlight, and the trigger was never squeezed.

"Uncle Talt died with a broken heart. He thought Bad John had double-crossed him."

John had it both ways and all ways. When most of his adversaries were dead and he was too old to enjoy the delights of venery he hearkened to the voice of the preachers. A weekly newspaper reported to his "many friends in Letcher County" that John had "repented of his sins and been saved." He was baptized in confirmation of the same and—according to many—entered into the joys of everlasting life when he breathed his last on January 30, 1931.

The old feudist died without suspecting that his cabin at the head of Elkhorn Creek had once sheltered a youth who would become president of the United States.

Andrew J. May, a Prestonsburg Democrat, was elected to Congress in 1932 when the Roosevelt-Garner ticket ended a twelve-year Republican reign. He remained in the House for fourteen years until a charge of corruption sent him to the same federal penitentiary that once harbored his predecessor, John A. Langley. After he was paroled, he returned to the practice of law in his hometown. When I visited him there he told me about Franklin D. Roosevelt's experience with "Bad John."

During World War II May was chairman of the immensely important House Committee on Military Affairs. He went frequently to the White House to discuss the gigantic wartime proj-

161

ects Congress was called upon to authorize and finance. On one such occasion the president lit a cigarette, took a long puff, and exhaled a mighty cloud of smoke. Looking at May with his famous and infectious grin he astonished the congressman by asking, "Did you ever hear of 'Bad John' Wright?"

When May admitted that he had been personally acquainted with Wright, the commander-in-chief said that he had known him too. With no little gusto he described the circumstances.

Soon after the turn of the century the Delano and Roosevelt families acquired extensive land holdings in Harlan and Pike counties. The young FDR came to eastern Kentucky courthouses to abstract titles for his relatives. Old-timers remembered young Roosevelt as an avid listener to tale-tellers at county seat stores. They recalled, too, that when tobacco chewers spat on the glowing heating stoves, Roosevelt exuberantly did likewise. He could make a hot stove sizzle as well as the next man despite his lack of experience. In fact, he brought to the isolated backwoods county a new and surprising skill: he spat in a most elegant manner, a neat, precise stream between his prominent front teeth.

A fall night found the Harvard law student and his portly uncle on horses traveling from Harlan to Pikeville. There were no inns so they stopped at Bad John's place. He agreed to take them in, but warned that his house was already crowded with travelers seeking shelter from the chill autumn rains.

When bedtime came, John said that the only bed available was an extra one in the huge room where he and his wife slept. Wallace Delano had an unshakable habit of sleeping alone and refused to make an exception even in these exceptional circumstances. This reduced Franklin to a pallet on the rough floor in front of the fire.

The pallet was meager and the boards were hard. Presently his uncle began to snore and Franklin feigned slumber. Bad John raised himself up and looked about at the shadowy room, satisfying himself that his guests were in deep repose. Thereupon he began "taking liberties" with Mrs. Wright. These proceedings continued for a quarter of an hour or longer. When they had been successfully concluded John fell back and began to snore with a vigor that matched Delano's. All night long, FDR told the congressman, the two snored at each other in booming cannonades of raucous sound. FDR rose as weary as when he retired.

The next morning the dutiful Mrs. Wright fed them a fine breakfast of ham, eggs, biscuits, apple butter, and coffee. John gave them an "eye-opener" of moonshine whiskey and sold them a quart for their saddlebags. He charged them a dollar each for their accommodations.

FDR grinned and his eyes twinkled with the good humor that made him an unbeatable candidate and a great president. "I am probably the only man in the world who ever watched Bad John Wright make love," he concluded. The architect of the New Deal, the Great Arsenal of Democracy, and the Grand Alliance laughed mischievously at the recollection.

The Ghost of
the Czar

MONROE LUCAS was born on Camp Branch in Letcher County in 1878. He had the slight build, distinguished features, and perpetual courtesy of the natural patrician. His whimsy and good humor were deeply ingrained, and I never saw him when he was not smiling.

When he was fifteen he read an advertisement that changed his life. The Chicago School of Magic and Ventriloquy was offering a correspondence course. For a mere thirty dollars payable in eight weekly installments, a subscriber could receive in the mail eight easy-to-follow lessons. By reading the simple instructions and practicing a few hours each day he could learn numerous sleight-of-hand tricks and the "fundamentals of magic." Furthermore, he could learn "to project his voice and master the ancient art of the ventriloquist." Monroe had thirty dollars earned from the sale of ginseng and mayapple roots and other herbs, and he swallowed the bait. In secrecy he sent his money and received his lessons. Fear of ridicule prompted him to keep his undertaking entirely to himself. Each lesson was carefully studied and practiced, then stored in a box concealed in his father's fodder loft.

Monroe told me that he "took to the lessons like a duck takes to water." His fingers were slender, supple, and quick, and he was able to follow the illustrations almost from the first. He had a nimble Irish tongue that poured out a disconcerting patter of the kind recommended by the masters in Chicago. He spent long hours at his task, most of them in a shallow cave at the top of a hill. Here he was out of sight and hearing, and none could belittle him and his plans to "be a magician."

He barely contained himself from one week to the next. He found the instructions completely fascinating. The greatest challenge was the ventriloquism, but this too came naturally. He learned to form his words normally, the breath being released slowly, his tongue retracted and only the tip in motion. He spoke with his mouth open only slightly and the glottis narrowed. From this rearranging of his speaking habits came words that seemed to emanate from stones, stumps, and such other items as were near at hand when he practiced. He spent so many hours on the hilltops and behaved so strangely that his parents became concerned. His father thought he was "acting crazy," and his mother suspected that he had fallen in love. But they were equally astounded by the results of his curious furtiveness. After the last lesson had been digested and assimilated and the box with its precious contents safely hidden, Monroe decided that the time had come to test his new skill on the unsuspecting people along Rock House Creek.

The family was preparing for bed on a rainy night in October. The cat was curled up on the hearth when Mr. Lucas decided to eject him. He opened the door and called, but the sleepy Tom did not respond. Irritated, and sleepy himself, the master of the house put his foot behind the animal and gave him a rude shove toward the door. The yellow cat dashed into the darkness and said in a small, clear voice, "You'll regret that!"

Monroe's father stopped in mid-step as if turned to stone. His mouth open, his eyes popping, he stood unmoving for eight or ten seconds. Then he put his foot down and followed the disgruntled cat into the rainy blackness. Monroe heard him blundering around in the yard calling "kitty, kitty, kitty," in a voice of quavering entreaty. At last he stumbled up the steps with the cat in his arms and placed him gently in the same spot he had previously occupied. He looked at the cat for a long moment, his eyes narrowed, his right hand reflectively stroking his chin. Then the cat settled down for another nap and, as his eyes closed, said quite distinctly, "Thank you, Mr. Lucas!"

For several days Monroe's father was a harried soul if one ever lived. He ate little and slept poorly. He had virtually nothing to say, and when spoken to seemed to rouse himself from a deep study about some remote matter. He shunned the cat but made absolutely certain he did nothing to disturb the creature. His wife made him a tonic of molasses, water, bitterroot, and a mammoth slug of moonshine whiskey. After he swallowed the powerful mixture, he went straight to bed, pulled up the cover, and began to snore. Then he stirred, sat up, and yelled, "Don't put the cat out! No matter what happens, don't put the cat out!" A moment later his frayed nerves collapsed in the sweet balm of sleep.

The boy's new skill provided him immense pleasure. He guarded his secret jealously, improving it any time he found himself alone. Camp Branch began to teem with dogs, chickens, cats, cows, and mules that occasionally delivered themselves of oral profundities. No one noticed that Monroe Lucas was always present when the creatures became talkative. Such incidents never failed to stir a major response, however, as when "Black Rob" Bates undertook to sell Monroe's father a saddle horse. Black Rob said the animal was young, sound of wind, and well trained. But the horse did not want to be sold under false assurances and spoke right up in the middle of the negotiations. "Tell him the truth, Mr. Bates. I'm as old as you are!"

In those days every ablebodied man was required to labor on the county roads five days out of each year, or hire a substitute to do his stint for him. The county judge appointed a road superviser in each voting precinct to see that the men turned out and made the needed improvements. The judge was astounded into speechlessness when the level-headed Republican he had designated for the Polly precinct explained why no work had been accomplished on the Camp Branch road. "You see, judge, it was this way. I had a big gang of men all turned out with tools and ready to go. They got set to dig and Shade Sexton hauled off with a sledgehammer and hit a big rock with all his might. When he done that, the rock yelled, 'Oh!' It was plain to hear. Ever' man there heard it, including me. Well, he hit it again and it said, 'Oh Lord,' and sounded real mad. Shade dropped his hammer and as soon as it hit the ground it said, pitiful like, 'Don't leave me here!' Judge, when the hammer said that, the men scattered in all directions and the milishy couldn't drive 'em back to work. They'd die first. "

When I knew Monroe he was an old man and had earned his living for many years with two little "dummies" named Rastus and Lizy. He carried them in a battered leather case and was a familiar sight in a score of eastern Kentucky and West Virginia counties. He was a born entertainer and the dummies delighted people of all ages along countless creeks. Even in the bleakest years of the depression when most were fortunate to earn a couple of dollars daily on relief projects, Monroe, Rastus, and Lizy could attract a crowd with enough dimes and nickels to fill his pockets. "People had mighty little to laugh about in those days, and many were sick with pessimism. It made me feel good all over to get a crowd of people interested in my tricks and to hear them haw-haw. Sometimes the little skinny, half-starved children would roll in the floor because of the smart-alecky things my dummies said to them, laughing until they were breathless. I like to think this helped all the people I entertained to feel better about their lives and to realize that better days would come. "

Many people thought Monroe was a witch and that his dummies were the work of the devil. They had lived in such benumbing isolation and were so steeped in superstition that the talking dummies appeared sinister, explicable only in terms of the supernatural. One of his neighbors told me that he always killed Monroe's cats because they "spied on" him and then

167

"went and told Lucas" all that he said and did. Monroe described an outrage that was committed against his beloved Rastus by a mountaineer in Logan County, West Virginia. The crowd had gathered at the local schoolhouse on a summer evening and Monroe was in good form as the hundreds of eyes followed his hands and listened to the banter of the two little personalities on his lap. Their eyes rolled in mock wrath, their legs kicked at one another, their mouths opened to reveal huge white teeth. Through it all they quarreled with each other and with Monroe. Rastus became obstreperous and told Monroe to watch his language. He demanded half the money taken in at the performance and said Lizy was not entitled to any of it. In fact, he said he intended to divorce Lizy and demanded to know whether there was a judge in the house. Monroe talked to him with the gentle reasonableness of a kindly father, urging marital reconciliation and advising Rastus not to be greedy for money. He proposed that Rastus accept twenty-five cents with Monroe keeping the rest. Lizy complained that she had nowhere to go and that divorce would leave her stranded by the roadside, shelterless and pitiful. Rastus rejected Monroe's good counsel and suggested that they change roles. He would get a big leather case and put Monroe and Lizy into it. Then he, Rastus, would carry them about with him to performances. He would give Monroe a quarter and keep the rest of the money, and that way Monroe would have to endure being shut up with the unbearable Lizy all day.

The crowd relished the exchange, or at least most of them did. One elderly mountaineer was far from pleased, however. When the session ended he came forward with a sturdy switch he had cut from a nearby birch. "I'd wear that little devil out right now if I was you. The way he talked back to you here among all these people was a disgrace and you ought not to put up with it! "

From inside the carrying case came a frightened voice. "Please don't whip me. I didn't mean no harm! "

The mountaineer was jubilant. He handed Monroe the

switch. "You see, he is already straightening around. The next time you take him out of that satchel show him this limb, and you'll have no more trouble with him!"

On another trip to his "neighbors in West Virginia" a crowd gathered in a movie theater at Kermit. The irrepressible Rastus went too far and almost got himself killed. Prominent among the audience was a young man with a handsome country girl on his arm. The swain was rigged up in a blue serge suit and gray ankle spats. Fluffy sideburns adorned his cheeks, and his lips and chin were hidden by whiskers and a bristly black mustache. His face was locked in a fierce, self-important scowl which Monroe's performance could not relax. His girl friend, though, joined in the general laughter and applause and seemed disappointed when her companion remained unamused.

At last Monroe became nettled. Rastus caught sight of the bearded face for the first time and fell back in terror. Monroe asked what had frightened him and Rastus quavered, "That man has swallowed a mule." Monroe demanded to know why Rastus had said so strange a thing, reminding him that it was impossible for a man to swallow a mule. Rastus took another look and replied, "I know he swallowed a mule 'cause its tail is hanging out of his mouth!"

The entire crowd—including the young lady—dissolved in laughter. The bearded youth blushed beneath the whiskers and sideburns and glared malevolently at the dummy. His obvious discomfiture was the funniest part of the evening but the humorless oaf thought otherwise. He headed for Rastus, vowing to tear him apart on the spot. Fortunately the town marshal was close at hand and Rastus was saved. He apologized for his remark, and probably made matters worse with, "I was wrong about him. He didn't swallow a mule. He just looks like he swallowed a mule."

The exasperated girl left without her escort, and the marshal accompanied Monroe and the chastened Rastus to their hotel room. On a later trip to Kermit, the marshal informed him that Rastus's victim appeared on the street next day minus sideburns, mustache, and chin whiskers. Sometime after that he married the girl.

Monroe's jovial eyes twinkled as he told me about an episode that took place on Millstone Creek when he was about twenty. In those days, he said, most people were gullible beyond belief, and newspapers played on their innocence with accounts of outlandish and preposterous happenings. These reports gave the bored people something to talk about and instilled in each reader the hope that the next incredible event would befall *him*.

Monroe's cousin had taken a wife and in due course had begotten a son. The birth of this red-faced, wrinkled little character was greeted with unrestrained joy by the triumphant father, who immediately rode across the ridge to spread the joyous tidings. He urged Monroe to come see the heir and congratulate the happy mother.

Monroe went on Sunday, when the newcomer was one week old. The two grandmothers were there to do the housework for a few days and the proud mother sat in a circle of admiring relatives with the baby curled happily asleep in her arms. Blood relationships were extremely important to mountaineers and they remarked on supposed family resemblances. One of the grandmothers took a fresh look and vowed that he looked "exactly like his pap." This brought the other grandmother for a reinspection, after which she declared, " 'Pears like he is the image of his ma." Amid these activities the baby stirred, waved its tiny arms and hands, opened its minuscule pink lips and said in a thin but audible voice, "I'm hungry."

There were a dozen people in the room, including the old "granny-woman" midwife who had dragged the infant into the world in the first place. All had heard the two words so there could be absolutely no doubt on that point. The week-old child had informed them that he was hungry. A minute or more passed in utter silence, then "pap" got his wits together and broke the spell. Addressing his wife in a stern tone of husbandly authority he commanded, "You heard what he said. Go ahead and feed him!"

All agreed that this was a singularly wise course to take, and amid a babble of such excited chatter as had never been heard before on Millstone Creek the mother exposed an ample breast and pressed the nipple into the baby's mouth. He pulled at the flowing fount for a few seconds, then released it. "This milk is too warm," he complained.

The crowd scattered. Up the creek and down the creek, across the ridges and into the hollows the tale spread. A dozen eye witnesses passed the word to incredulous stay-at-homes. Those who heard did not hesitate to place their hands on Bibles and swear to the truth of it all. The Lucas baby became the talk of the valley and surrounding valleys. The midwife said the child was "forward"; she had recognized that immediately. He was like Moses and other outstanding children described in the Bible. Undoubtedly the good Lord had chosen this baby to grow up and do important things. The grandparents agreed at once, sagely noting signs of greatness in every limb and feature. One of the grandfathers calculated the boy would get rich "like John D. Rockefeller." This hopeful prophecy caused the neighbors to treat the entire household with reverence, even awe. Having a future John D. Rockefeller for a neighbor was a marvelous thing to contemplate, and the contemplation brought numerous new insights into everyone who had had any role whatever in the production of the baby.

Several times in later days the little one addressed his admiring elders. Once he admonished them to be quiet. The next day a bluetick hound followed his master inside the house and was kicked out the door when the baby said, "Get that hound out of here!" The father, too, received rough treatment when his tiny son told a crowded room, "Pap's been drinkin' moonshine agin.'"

A stock drover carried the word to Lexington where it came to the attention of a reporter for the *Lexington Herald*. By train to Jackson and by rented horse the rest of the way he journeyed to Whitesburg. There he enlisted the aid of Nehemiah Webb, publisher and editor of the local weekly, the *Mountain Eagle*, and they made their way together to the Lucas household. By chance Monroe was there for a visit when the two reporters arrived to "see the talking baby."

The four grandparents, the ever-vigilant "granny-woman," the parents, cousin Monroe, and the two reporters gathered about the phenomenal child. At first he slept, silent and unmoving. Then he stirred and took some milk, after which he inquired, "Who are these two strangers?" Mr. Webb explained with all the dignity he could muster in speaking to one so insignificant in size. The baby then announced, "I don't like newspaper reporters," and went back to sleep.

The people left after that, the two newsmen the object of dark looks from the grandparents. If their grandson didn't like reporters, neither did they.

In the yard the *Lexington Herald* reporter tapped Monroe on the shoulder and steered him a little distance away to the shade of an apple tree. "Lucas," he demanded, "where in the hell did you learn ventriloquism? That was a damn good act you put on in there!"

Monroe confessed, and the others were startled when the "man from Lexington" threw his head back and laughed as if he had heard the greatest joke in history. Then he squeezed Monroe's arm in reassurance and whispered, "I'll never tell a soul. You've got too good a thing going here and, besides, these people couldn't stand the shock. They would wither and die if they learned that the baby can't talk."

Sixty years had passed when Monroe told me about the "forward baby." "What became of him?" I inquired. "Nothing," he replied. "He never amounted to a hill of beans." And then with a super twinkle, "He never said another word till he was nearly three years old."

When Monroe was forty-five, he became tired of traveling around with his shows and got a job for a while as a miner. He worked for Elk Horn Coal Company on Thornton Creek. Floyd Mercer was the mine superintendent and he set Monroe to loading coal with a huge "red edge" shovel. The coal was hauled out in cars pulled by mules. The driver in Monroe's section was named Goins and at the end of Monroe's first shift Goins quit. He was notorious for his cruel treatment of the mules but after that day he avoided all "work stock" as if the animals carried a deadly plague. Mercer said Goins explained his departure from the employ of Elk Horn Coal Company as follows:

"Mercer, I quit as of now. I ain't takin' no chance with no more mules, no time and no place!"

Mercer was mystified, but Goins enlightened him. "That old brown mule, Beck, got tangled up in the traces and when I went to straighten them out he kicked at me. I slapped him over the end of the nose and cussed him a little, and he curled his lips back and I could see his big yaller teeth. Then he said to me as plain as anything I ever heard in my life, 'If you don't treat me better I will tell the Angel of Death, and he will drop you alive into hell!' He looked me square in the eye when he said it."

Was anyone else there, Mercer asked, but Goins hadn't taken time to look for witnesses. He had brought that mule outside and combed and brushed him from end to end. He had given him fresh water and abundant oats, plus hay and corn fodder. But he was through with mules after today.

Mercer was at his wit's end. "You surely don't believe in talking mules," he argued.

"I don't believe in talkin' mules in general, but I sure as hell believe in that particular talkin' mule," was the unwavering reply.

Mercer tried once more. "Well, anyway, the mule didn't say for you to quit working for us. He said for you to start treating him better. You've already started doing that, so you're safe!"

But Goins was adamant. "I know that I'm treating him better. You know that I'm treating him better. The Lord in heaven knows I'm treating him better. But that mule may not know I'm treating him better, and I ain't takin' no chances!"

The last time Monroe came to my office he was well above eighty. After seeking my opinion concerning some property he was selling, he told me about a ghost that terrorized the Rock House Creek territory of Letcher County in those long-gone times when he was an agile sixteen.

A revival preacher had been there and stirred up the people with fiery sermons about the agonizing manner in which Satan would dispose of sinners in the last days. And the last days were near, with "nation arming against nation" in preparation for Armageddon. "Be ready," he shouted, "for you know not the day nor the hour!" He urged them to go out into their yards at night and watch the skies for "signs" of the Second Coming. Suddenly young and old alike were meditating on these dire warnings and gazing into the starlit heavens. The more they looked, the more apprehensive they became, for the sky was streaked with multitudes of "falling stars" and other signals of divine wrath. While this mood lay heavy on the land, Monroe and a couple of his friends decided to give the people a "sign" they would never forget.

A pair of immense black turkey buzzards roosted in a cliff near the head of the valley. On warm bright days they could be seen circling for hours, their outstretched wings carrying them round and round in the ascending air currents. On a Saturday afternoon the three conspirators made their way to the rocky aerie. They carried with them a curious collection of items: an old fishing net, some strings, and a white union suit—a discarded undergarment once worn by Monroe's father to ward off the icy blasts of winter. They were unlikely objects indeed to carry to a sun-blistered crag on one of the hottest days of the year.

The buzzards had built a nest in a cleft, and there amid the twigs and leaves the female sat on the huge eggs. Before the awkward creature could start, the net entangled her and she was a prisoner. She pecked, clawed, and scratched but the boys held

174

fast, sometimes having to fend off the outraged male who shared her indignation at this unprecedented invasion. As night approached, their work proceeded as planned and the valley was about to be shaken by a major "sign."

The strings were tied securely to the wrists of the long-sleeved and long-legged underwear. Then at the other end the strings were affixed to the kicking legs of the buzzard hen. The front of the garment was unbuttoned and the burdened and protesting fowl was carried to the topmost pinnacle of the crag. Darkness fell and a full moon rode high above the southern horizon. The stars were innumerable and brilliant, and not even a wisp of cloud was visible. People had eaten supper and were gathered in groups, their eyes fastened on the distant stars. The elders told youngsters that the moon was the "lesser light" that God had set in the sky to light their path at night just as the sun, "the greater light," illumined the day for their especial benefit. The graybeards chilled them, too, with warnings that soon an angel would come and set one foot on the land and one foot on the sea and "declare that time will be no more." There was talk about the glories of heaven, and then the inevitable drift carried them to the devil and his satanic kingdom of hell. Little ones, already quaking because of the imminent end of it all, were terrified to learn that Satan was everywhere all the time and could "carry off sinners" within a flicker of an eyelash. As the gloomy discussions continued in one family gathering after another, the three lads on the cliff prepared to release their prisoner.

The net was taken from about her mighty wings. The tattered union suit was wadded up in a ball under her feet. Suddenly she and the garment were flung upward and outward from the rock peak and the coal black, hideous fowl flapped her wings and sped away, determined to put as much distance as possible between herself and her tormentors.

As she flew, the ancient "long johns" billowed beneath her. Air filled the seat, the legs, and the arms, and the curiously shaped bag pulled her down and slowed her flight. As her black pinions beat the air, her legs kicked up and down in a frantic ef-

175

fort to shake off the impediment. The wings made an indescribable muffled sound, somewhat like that of a high wind beating through a dense hedge or thicket. The distracted bird cried out in terror, or tried to, and her erratic journey was accompanied by a "whuck! whuck! whuck!" that carried far and wide on the dry summer air.

She headed toward the west, a vast darkness of flailing wings carrying a frantically agitated, shroud-encased body. The apparition flew nearly the entire length of the valley and was seen by a score of sky-watching congregations—young, old, and middle-aged. The dreadful sign was unmistakably clear—Satan was carrying a doomed soul to the pit and the piteous gurgling cries of the unfortunate wretch filled their ears. The sign foretold by the revival preacher had been manifested to them. Time was short, and the people along Rock House Creek could repent or take the consequences.

The next day an imaginative soul told an unnerved gathering that he had seen it all. He thought he might have an explanation. According to the newspapers the old and wicked czar of Russia had just died after a lifetime of bloodthirsty oppression. The whole world had been shocked by his iniquities. At his death the Lord had given the world a sign. The people along Rock House Creek had been watching and they saw it. They were the fortunate ones.

Old heads nodded sagely and the explanation spread, gaining credence and acceptance at every telling. It was natural, even inevitable that a wicked king should receive special treatment when God required his last breath. Sinful king and sinful commoner shared the same hell, but it was only right that the former should be ushered there in a more dramatic fashion.

The ghost of the czar made a tremendous impression and set off a new round of revivals and scores of "conversions." Uncountable sins were confessed, and many went to the baptizing holes. Moonshining and lechery lost their charms for a while.

A squirrel hunter found a curious object on a high cliff on Thornton Creek. Something had carried an old union suit to the top of the crag known as Herod's Rock and had torn it to shreds. The sleeves had once been tied with tough sea-grass cord but this, too, had been frayed to ravelings. Caught in the pathetic ruin of this once-splendid garment were a couple of coarse black feathers.

I asked Monroe whether Rastus and Lizy were still talkative, and he said they were not. They went to sleep about eight or ten years ago, he thought, and had not been out of their case since. "One night my wife and I were at home alone and I got the dummies out and held them on my lap. They called her 'mother' and said she had been wonderfully good to them, and to Monroe. They told her that she had treated her stepchildren born of Monroe's first marriage with so much kindness that they loved her more than they did their own father, so that when they came for visits they always hugged and kissed her before they even said hello to him. They said that this was only right because a mother's work and love are more important and longer lasting than a father's. Rastus said 'Monroe loves you as much as we do, but he is too bashful to say so!'

"Then they told her 'good night' and went back to sleep."